FEMININE NATION

Performance, Gender and Resistance in the Works of John McGahern and Neil Jordan

Lori Rogers

University Press of America,® Inc.
Lanham • New York • Oxford

Copyright © 1998 by
University Press of America,® Inc.
4720 Boston Way
Lanham, Maryland 20706

12 Hid's Copse Rd.
Cummor Hill, Oxford OX2 9JJ

All rights reserved
Printed in the United States of America
British Library Cataloging in Publication Information Available

Library of Congress Cataloging-in-Publication Data

Rogers, Lori.
Feminine nation : performance, gender, and resistance in the works
of John McGahern and Neil Jordan / Lori Rogers
p. cm.
Includes bibliographical references and index.
1. McGahern, John, 1934—Criticism and interpretation. 2.
Feminism and literature—Ireland—History—20th century. 3.
English fiction—Irish authors—History and criticism. 4. English
fiction—20th century—History and criticism. 5. Jordan, Neil,
1951- — Criticism and interpretation. 6. National characteristics,
Irish, in literature. 7. Femininity (Psychology) in literature. 8.
Women—Ireland—History—20th century. 9. Sex role in literature.
10. Ireland—In literature. 11. Women in literature. I. Title.
PR6063.A2176Z86 1997   820.9'352042—DC21   97-41212 CIP

ISBN 0-7618-0950-3 (cloth: alk. ppr.)
ISBN 0-7618-0951-1 (pbk: alk. ppr.)

The paper used in this publication meets the minimum
requirements of American National Standard for information
Sciences—Permanence of Paper for Printed Library Materials,
ANSI Z39.48—1984

For Jimba, Andrew, Nicholas
and
for Peter

Contents

Preface

Acknowledgments

Introduction	**De-colonization and de-programming**	1
Chapter 1	**Engendering the post-colonial**	19
Chapter 2	**Break up the family**	35
Chapter 3	**Courting performance: coercion and compromise**	59
Chapter 4	**The private performance: domestic women's resistance**	77
Chapter 5	**Going through the change: poison in the well**	105
Conclusion		125
Bibliography		135
Index		149

Preface

The number of scholarly books published on Anglo-Irish literature each year is astonishing when one considers that the majority of them are concerned with writing from Ireland since 1800. The not-quite two centuries that Ireland has produced prose fiction and poetry might seem to provide a very shallow literary tradition when compared to literature from England or even the United States. The lumping together of Anglo-Irish and American literature under the rubric of English literature (which should of course mean solely literature from England) reinforces Ireland's subordinate literary history. The reason that most critical studies of literature from Ireland do focus on literature after 1800 is that it is in the nineteenth century that the transition from Irish literature (in Irish) to Anglo-Irish literature (in English) takes place. So it seems logical that Anglo-Irish literature would be viewed as a subset of English literature, and studied in that light.

But, of course, Anglo-Irish literature's popularity is not defined by its relative youth or supposed ancillary nature. Because of the strong political identification readers have with Ireland, whether they read in sympathy with Ireland's long and well-publicized struggles for independence or in spite of them, literature from Ireland has always carried a double weight, being assigned a literary value almost secondarily to an historical, socio-political value which is more immediately upfront than in the other "English" literatures.

Many Anglo-Irish writers have of course used this political charge to advance political theories in their writing, and studies of these theories contribute to the large number of critical books on Anglo-Irish literature. The fascination with the Ireland and its literature stems in part from its combination of political danger and cultural safety—to many Ireland represents all the interesting dilemmas of post-colonialism and nation-building presented within the safe context of a familiar, white, western nation which, because of the Irish diaspora since the nineteenth century, so many people consider themselves to be part of. The effects of British colonialism on the many other nations besides Ireland who experienced them remain shrouded in darkness compared to the spotlight trained on the troubled history of England's nearest colony. In fact, Ireland's well-studied past looms so large that it sometimes seems to represent a unique experience. But the benefits of comparative analyses of Ireland's and other nations' colonial and post-colonial experience are invaluable, and open up badly-needed new avenues of exploration into Ireland's literature, culture, and role in world politics.

The fact that the future so rarely plays a part in the construction of theories and readings of Anglo-Irish literature is striking. What I would like this book to do is present a study of contemporary Anglo-Irish literature which shows that literature interacting with the society that gives it context and shaping that society even as it has been shaped, and therefore impacting the shape of things to come. The focus of this book is on contemporary Anglo-Irish as a post-colonial literature working out the same problems as many other post-colonial literatures around the world, with a special focus on gender issues and women's roles in becoming citizens in the modern nation. Whereas there are many hundreds of books available on gender and nation-building in other post-colonial nations, this remains an issue which has not been popular with Anglo-Irish scholars in general until recently, and as yet there are too few books devoted to studying gender oppression and construction in Ireland and its literature. If this book can make a contribution to the future by adding to the ranks of full-length studies of gender and feminism in Anglo-Irish literature and paving the way for more, then it will have done its work.

Acknowledgements

First, thanks go to the members of my original dissertation committee, Krin Gabbard, Sandy Petrey, Ilona Rashkow and Tim Brennan. When their input and continued help over the years are taking into consideration, this book seems a collaborative effort.

Peter Stokes exerted all his critical and encouraging powers on me and this book without complaint, and is certainly deserving of all my thanks and regard.

I thank Tim Gaherty for innumerable years of support and insight which were crucial to my work on this project and more.

My family, Jim, Irene, Jim, Kathie, Jim, Andrew and Nicholas, provided invaluable support from a long distance.

Claudia Montilla, Pamela Moore and Shailja Sharma made my life in Comparative Literature fruitful in a number of ways, intellectually, spiritually and companionably. I am their inheritor in many ways.

Jean, Jim, Helen and Eric Keegan, Paula Haines and Karyn Valerius were all invaluable to my health and well-being during my years at Stony Brook, and will continue to be so long into the future.

Permission to reprint from *The Past*, first published by Jonathan Cape Ltd. 1980 © Neil Jordan 1980, from Lutyens & Rubenstein.

From *Amongst Women* by John McGahern. Copyright © 1990 by John McGahern. Used by permission of Viking Penguin, a division of Penguin Books USA Inc.

Permission to reprint from *The Dream of A Beast* and *The Crying Game* from *A NEIL JORDAN READER* by Neil Jordan. Copyright © 1993 by Neil Jordan. Reprinted by permission of Vintage Books, a Division of Random House Inc.

Introduction

De-colonization and de-programming

> History is a nightmare from which I am trying to awake.
> --James Joyce

> A normal literature, while welcoming the criticism of outsiders neither lives nor dies by such criticism. It abides the judgement of its own people, and by that judgement lives or dies (Taylor 1969, 6).
> --Daniel Corkery

In his introduction to *Nationalism, Colonialism and Literature*, Seamus Deane comments on a monotony concerning those three topics in relation to Ireland.[1] It is

> inevitable monotony, inescapable in colonial conditions. What seems like an endless search for a lost communal or even personal identity is doubly futile. Just naming it indicates that it is lost; once named, it can never be unnamed. [Such] an identification is wholly unreal...made manifest only by pretending it is the conclusion to a search of which it was the origin. (Deane 1986, 11)

Deane's complaint is a valid one, with which most students of Anglo-Irish literature would concur.[2] This monotony accompanying Irish studies is the end result of reading a multitude of claims and counter-claims to the "truth about the Irish." It is composed of myriad attempts to identify once and for all what "Irishness" is and what it should be and who is authorized by blood or law to represent that identity. The quest for "Irishness" takes up a great deal of the time and energy of Ireland's writers and critics, and creates a fork in the road for the reader whereat she must either stop reading or espouse a particular theory. Side-taking is Anglo-Irish literature's ultimate demand on its readers.

If the reader is able to avoid side-taking, which leads inevitably to a more or less tedious involvement in the endless minutiae of Irish history and literary history and theory of literature and history, she will be able to look at Anglo-Irish literature in a context other than patriotic. She will see Anglo-Irish literature as affect and effect of pre- and post-colonial nation-building, similar in this respect to other literatures from countries once part of the British Empire. India, Jamaica, Nigeria and Canada, to name a very few, are nations which share a common literary/colonial history with Ireland. Catherine Innes, in *The Devil's Own Mirror: The Irishman and African in Modern Literature*, illustrates the similarities between Irish and African literary politics:

> Black and Irish writers [both] sought to identify with a national or ethnic group and to express its culture and characteristics...to affirm that culture in reaction to previous devaluation and repression...to define their groups as a people worthy of self-government, and to do so fashioned or revived a form and style which might speak for and to the oppressed group. [The] emphasis on "soul" in African peoples is comparable to the insistence on "emotional warmth" and spirituality as the mark of the true Celt. Both groups claim to be more humane, more in tune with the elemental and natural, more vital and less alienated than the Anglo-Saxon or European, whose culture is denounced as mechanistic and artificial. ...African and Gaelic cultures are both considered most authentic when associated with music, dance and the spoken word. (Innes 1990, 5-6)

Comparative studies such as Innes' are rare in Irish studies.[3] Irish historians and critics, for the most part, refuse to see themselves as part of a larger post-colonial context. On the back cover of David Lloyd's book on nineteenth-century Anglo-Irish studies Denis Donoghue, the arch-canonical Irish critic, states that Lloyd's placing of Yeats, Beckett, Heaney "and other writers" into "the context of cultural studies and minorities' [sic] discourse" is a gauntlet thrown to Irish criticism: "We must take serious issue with [Lloyd]" (Lloyd 1993, back cover). The drive to keep Irish colonial and post-colonial experience exclusively Irish has been a strong, single-minded and successful one. Many scholars within Irish studies have tried hard to give Ireland's political experiences the appearance of singularity, succeeding to the point where, ironically, few outside the field of Irish studies are particularly interested in it.

The cases of Joyce, Yeats, Beckett, Shaw and Behan (to add a few to Donoghue's list) are evidence of the fruits of Irish isolationism, which sets up questing for Irishness as the writer's most important task and drives away those who do not conform to that task in a manner deemed appropriate.[4] These authors are among the few Irish writers who have some measure of renown outside Irish studies circles. Yet they spent their lives outside Ireland and are readily subsumed into English or World Literature. Joyce's works represent "the Irish People" to most of the world outside Ireland, yet it is well-known that his books were not well-received (or received at all) in his native land, but angrily discounted as negative criticism of the traditional Celticism which was the national critical ideology. Joyce is now recuperated, of course, along with the others mentioned, but the critical situation in Irish studies has not changed a great deal since 1904. Traditional, compassionate representations of the Irish are still favored over more fractured interpretations of identity, while Irishness and how best to uphold it against foreign influences are still the focal points of concern for most Anglo-Irish critics.

What I want to do in this study is to deliberately explore that "context of cultural studies and minorities' discourse" that so threatens Heaney and other proponents of traditional Irish studies. This study situates two contemporary Anglo-Irish novelists--Neil Jordan and John McGahern--within the socio-political culture of the post-colonial Republic of Ireland and documents some of the effects of this specific cultural milieu of twentieth-century nation-building on their writing. Before focusing on these two writers, however, the culture of Anglo-Irish literature, especially the novel, and then the culture of post-colonial self-image must first be described.

Criticism, Irishness and the Anglo-Irish Novel

> Whereas the island has an enviable canon of literature, a critical canon would be difficult to conjure into existence (Foster 1987, 10).

> Irishness is not primarily a question of birth or blood or language; it is the condition of being involved in the Irish situation, and usually of being mauled by it (Foster 1987, 10).
> --Conor Cruise O'Brien

Focusing on contemporary Anglo-Irish prose fiction is the first irregular move this study makes, in light of the Anglo-Irish novel's negative reception by proponents of those interrelated Anglo-Irish critical institutions, nationalism and Irishness. The Anglo-Irish novel has always taken third place in importance behind the powerhouses of poetry and drama, and the contemporary novel has enjoyed even less esteem than products of the fragmented and halting novel tradition of the nineteenth century. John Wilson Foster states that "whereas the poetry and drama of the Irish literary revival have been studied broadly and in-depth, the movement's achievements in fiction have been neglected...The revival encouraged other literary forms at [the novel's] expense" (Foster 1987, xi).[5] Of nineteenth-century Anglo-Irish novelists, only Edgeworth, Somerville, Ross, and Moore stand out as writers of consistent talent, and Somerville, Ross and especially Moore all wrote into the twentieth century. William Carleton is often recruited to swell the thin ranks of nineteenth-century novelists although he was primarily a short-story writer. Yet twentieth-century critics insist on the supremacy of the previous century's novel. In *The Irish Novelists: 1800-1850*, Thomas Flanagan states that the "nineteenth century Irish novel established no tradition," and Joyce appears to be the only writer in Flanagan's opinion who was able to fill the shoes of Carleton and the greats of the nineteenth century (Flanagan 1959, 333).

I believe this preferential treatment of nineteenth-century fiction writers stems in part from their situation within colonial Ireland. Ireland as the bent-yet-never-bowed victim of English oppression is still the most intriguing and least complicated literary trope for most critics; the nineteenth-century writers experienced colonialism first-hand, and wrote about it with varying levels of emotion. Flanagan embodies this position in his conclusion to *The Irish Novelists*:

> It was in the nineteenth century that Irishmen [sic] paused, in the midst of turbulence and anger, to take stock of their various and vivid culture...Of what they saw and felt the novels [are] the truest record. The foolish enthusiasms of Lady Morgan and the wisdom of Maria Edgewroth, Griffin's pride and Carleton's fury--it was all written down, as Yeats was to say, in a fiery shorthand, that it might never be forgotten. (Flanagan 1959, 340)

Such histrionic appreciation is not unique to Flanagan. Granted, there are wonderful pieces of fiction from the nineteenth century, but the consequence of their staying power has been years dedicated to the exhumation and preservation of the body of Ireland enslaved. Contemporary colonial struggle justifies such one- or two-dimensional characters as Rory O'More and Glorvina and Sean O'Casey, who all fight for something.[6] Such characters and their patriotic sacrifices would perhaps be more objectively evaluated by contemporary critics and readers were it not for the continued importance of the colonial period in Irish schoolbooks and literature.[7] Colonial characters are meant to be read as eternal bearers and definers of Irishness. Their significance is never to become dated. The continuance of colonial struggle motifs into the twentieth century results in continued caricature-level celticism and patriotism in many contemporary Anglo-Irish novels. David Lloyd describes this situation as "the extreme demand for identification with the nation that nationalism imposes upon the Irish writer" and posits that the response of most Irish writers has been to try to create an Irish epic, necessarily colonial: "Both the popular and literary forms map a colonial culture for which the forms of representational politics and aesthetics required by nationalism begin to seem entirely inadequate, obliging us to conceive of a cultural politics which must work outside the terms of representation" (Lloyd 1993, 88).[8]

It is ironic that this demand for service to a national image forged during colonialism strives so often to elide the post-colonial in its contemporary manifestations. Even as the colonial era/experience is repeatedly validated within Anglo-Irish literature and criticism, debate rages as to whether the Republic of Ireland can be described as a post-colonial nation. Unfortunately, most of these arguments seem to base their resistance to the classification on racial lines: as there is no racial difference between the Irish and British, there could not have been any of the truly colonial discrimination against the Irish which other, non-white races encountered. This argument is outdated, as is evidenced by the work of Catherine Innes and many others, and utilizes narrow definitions of colonialism and race. Liam Kennedy's article "Modern Ireland: Post-Colonial Society or Post-Colonial Pretensions?" is an example of a well-argued yet basically flawed denial of Irish post-colonial status. Kennedy adopts a common-sense tone which inexplicably seems to identify "post-colonial" as a prestigious, even trendy label which serious theorists must relegate to "third world" nations. Because Ireland's GNP is greater than those of "real third-world" nations, Kennedy denies that a centuries-long history of colonial rule and rebellion in Ireland aligns Ireland with other nations subjected to foreign rule (Kennedy 1992/1993, 112). While I do not deny the differences between Irish colonial history and colonial history throughout the rest of the former British Empire, I also cannot deny Ireland's colonial history and necessarily post-colonial existence since 1916. Peadar Kirby's book *Has Ireland a Future?* is a convincing full-length comparative study of the similarities and differences between Irish and Latin American political structures which supports the premise that Ireland can be counted as a post-colonial society (Kirby 1988). Tellingly, Ireland's president, Mary Robinson, readily accepts the idea that Ireland is a post-colonial nation, "a mindset which she [has] defined as 'worrying uncertainty and self-deprecation'" (Mahoney 1993, 290). This controversial, non-insular definition of the nation by a woman is a point I will come back to below. So, because of the general fear of reducing Ireland to a "third world," non-white status, literature which treats Irish experience in the twentieth-century as post-colonial is given short shrift in an extremely effective way: it is simply not interpreted as such. That reading is made doggedly invisible by most critical interpretation. This study will try to overturn this rule of critical conduct.

For is not the obsession with "properly" expressing Irishness, a result of post-colonial identity building? The urge to assert the unique identity of a people which has suffered a colonizer's attempts at weakening that identity (cultural, political, linguistic) is strong in post-colonial societies and is a reasonable response to non-indigenous rule. And the Irish literary and critical culture manifests this consequence of new-found nationalism at every turn. Foster notes that "'expressing the Irish experience,' literature 'indigenous to and relative to Ireland'...express the same concept of an Irish dimension. In one form or another the concept is present in most discussions of Anglo-Irish writing...frequently seen in terms of nationality" (Foster 1987, 6). This is a capable summary of most critical stances both within and without Ireland, which rely on the yardstick of a text's or author's "Irishness quotient" to determine the worth of the text or author. A syllogism is at work: what keeps Ireland Irish, despite its intrinsic vagueness and openness to (often reliance on) subjective interpretations and value judgments, is Irishness itself. This Irishness is thus created as an insular entity, forged in the smithy of the Irish countryside rather than the international crucible of colonial politics and nation-building.

In this critical atmosphere, Ireland's novelists do not stand very tall. "It is of signal importance [that] the greatest of Ireland's novelists stood coldly aloof from the passions which the greatest of her [sic] poets had done so much to awaken," writes Flanagan (Flanagan 1959, 338-339). The impression that Anglo-Irish novelists, too prone to realism, are less Irish because of their "passionless objectivity" is common, although it is obviously no more than the continued expression of an old racial stereotype which defines the Irish as hot-blooded and irrational rather than objective and logical. Meanwhile, Joyce's passionate exposure of the Irish as just another average (or below-average) race of people is seen by the same critics as an insult to the nation. Yeats was largely responsible for popularizing the Irishness-as-merit school of criticism. "Yeats...[suggested] that this [Irish nationalist] literary enterprise would transcend political factions and create a sense of national unity for which the only adequate definition is spiritual," in which "cultural nationalism" would lead to establishment of a "transcendental [and indefinable] Irish essence" (Cairnes and Richards 1988, 65).

This then is the treacherous ground on which Anglo-Irish novelists are judged. Irishness is established as the joint creation of the critical and political establishments, definable as a mixture of popular feeling, traditional images of colonial anguish and anger, racial pride, bucolic celticism and state propaganda about the emotions and opinions of the "common Irish person." Ambiguous and ever-changing as this definition was, adherence to Irishness was quickly established during the Revival as the only measure of success of the Anglo-Irish writer. As Edna Longley puts it, "Irish canons have been...rough-hewn by indigenous axes...Revisionism is a shorthand and quasi-abusive term for historical studies held to be at odds with the founding ideology of the Irish Free State" (Longley 1994, 10). Estella Ruth Taylor notes the talented writer in Ireland is still largely to be identified on the basis of her ability to "represent significant Irish feeling and opinion" (Taylor 1969, 3).

Often "tone" is used as a synonym for Irishness; in "Double-Vision in Anglo-Irish Literature," Andrew Carpenter states that "tone is created by the writer himself [sic] and is a reflection of his person rather than his subject matter...[tone] is closely bound up with the way the writers look at things and this is...conditioned by the facts of Irish history and the realities of social and cultural attitudes in

Ireland" (Carpenter 1977, 113). This sort of personal experience construed as general representation is bound to happen when a writer is urged to experience Irishness firsthand in order to properly and fully extol its virtues. Rural writers were accepted as sources of true, unsullied celtic racial representation, and could publish their opinions to great acclaim. Others, more urbanly-challenged by their upbringing in the Pale, Cork or Belfast, repaired to the countryside to become more Irish and thus write the national epic. Synge's sojourn amongst the peasants is a well-known example of writers turning to the "more authentic" representatives of their race for inspiration. "True originality derives from the faithful reproduction of one's origins," or, in many cases, the faithful reproduction of one's mythic past through projection onto someone else's present (Lloyd 1993, 88). The murky criterion of "tone" obviously allows the critic a great deal of leeway for pseudo-psychoanalysis of text and author. Despite Carpenter's assertion, the tone generated by a text is not causally related to or reflective of the writer's soul; Kavanagh avowed hatred for Irishness but used the symbols of rural Ireland skillfully enough to be praised for the grassroots celticism of his tone and person. Edna O'Brien reveals the ugly underside of the lives of rural Irish women and is thus pilloried by Irish critics, yet she remains in rural Ireland, living much like the Irish country women she is said to have defamed.

Making a unified field theory of Irish ethnic feeling and opinion the basis of criticism has, of course, led to criticism

> distinguished by its highly personal and self-conscious tone produced by scattered statements of opinion, and [its] reflections and self-evaluations...a frequent approach to any writer is through the definition of the typical Irish character, and of the Irish mind, with the subsequent application of the definition to the individual author...in determining the validity of the writer's expression. (Taylor 1969, 3-4)

Within the format of this sort of criticism, which Longley describes as "Irish, Irisher, Irishest," (Longley 1994, 175), the novel, lengthy and involving many different possible "types" of characters, falls more easily prey to accusations of non-Irishness than the lyrically compact poem or stylized drama. Whereas the deviant play or poem has been written off as an anomaly, or, as in Beckett's case, as foreign, novels which question Irishness are seen to represent an evil symptomatic of the genre, and Anglo-Irish novelists who are renowned elsewhere are always late in receiving their critical due in Ireland.

The Irish critical canon too often seeks to explain this demand for Irishness of tone, content and intent as a sign that ancient Irish culture can be resumed in the modern era unscathed by centuries of colonization. The logic seems to be that if Ireland were really a post-colonial culture, it would have a fragmented self-image; therefore, producing uniform definitions and illustrations of Irishness is proof that there is no fragmentation. I will discuss below the ways in which this doctrine elides contrary readings, how, in short, texts which support readings that find evidence of fragmented national identity are simply read as if they did not.

So the student who comes to Anglo-Irish literature is faced with a closed circle, a literature absorbed by its own "exclusive" history and ethnic identity which demands a great deal of historical study before its grudges and name-dropping can be understood. The late twentieth-century reader must be familiar with the uprisings in Ulster of the sixties and seventies, the Free State of the thirties and forties, the civil war of teens and twenties, the uprising of 1916, Parnell, famine, Gratton, Wild Geese, the Penal Laws, and eight hundred years of colonial rule before then, stretching back to the first English plantation in 1169. Pre-history must be at one's command as well, repository as it is of the original pre-Christian celtic identity. "This obsession with nationalist history is familiar to students of Irish literature," comments James Cahalan in *Great Hatred, Little Room: The Irish Historical Novel*. "It is necessary to define the Irish historical novel, because if every Irish novel with history in it were to be included, just about every Irish novel ever written would have to be examined" (Cahalan 1983, xiii). Anglo-Irish fictions, along with Anglo-Irish critical works, have long explored the ways literary space merges with historical space, and what is meant to be objective reporting often becomes fictive and imaginative reliving of history (John Waters' *Jiving at the Crossroads* or William Thompson's *The Imagination of an Insurrection*) while what is meant as fiction becomes a text to found historical reality (Liam O'Flaherty's *Famine* or Elizabeth Bowen's *The Last September*). After beginning to incorporate the historical and literary-historical information behind contemporary Anglo-Irish literature, the reader soon realizes that she must either spend the greatest part of her energies solely on these issues of historicity and insular Irish identity (the well-beaten path) or break out of these conventions and study Anglo-Irish literature in a more comparative context.

New criticism: Post-Irishness Literary Theory

My study is of the latter kind. I intend to contextualize works by Jordan and McGahern within a different definition of "Irishness"-- in this case, Irishness, rather than meaning reliance upon cultural cliché or local color, will mean the representation of Irish experiences of nation-building after colonization. Irishness will not be a given, but will be de-constructed and examined critically as a set of complex, socio-political signifiers. This will help to move Irish studies outside its own insular tail-chasing into a comparative context which will invite the ideas of critics other than the usual Irish specialists.[9] I hope to provide the contemporary Anglo-Irish novel with some much-needed critical separation from Irish cultural tradition, to effect, as Longley puts it, a separation between cultural and political Irishness: "...to accelerate the separation between political 'Irishness' and culture in Ireland. Culture in Ireland is a range of practices, expressions, traditions, by no means homogeneously spread nor purely confined to the island. Political Irishness, on the other hand, is the ideology of identity [which serves] to bind the new state" (Longley 1994, 176). Literature is a political manifestation closely bound to and, of course, influential in developing and disseminating ideologies of national identity. Because of this, one cannot study Anglo-Irish literature as non-political cultural manifestation. And, in the case of Anglo-Irish literature, the political ideology in progress is bound up in the de-colonizing strategies of the state since 1916. I want to read McGahern's and Jordan's texts in a post-colonial context which is at once specifically Irish yet informed by a larger post-colonial context. So, although my focus is on that Irish society, the majority of this text is taken up by Anglo-Irish angles on life after Great Britain in the Irish Republic. But it will not be taken for granted that Ireland's experience of post-colonial nation-building and its effects on Anglo-Irish literature are unique to Ireland, but part of the larger, world-wide process of decolonization, and this approach should relieve the Anglo-Irish texts involved of the aura of ethnic exclusivity with which Irish Studies critics often surround them.

De-colonization and de-programming

For in any study of the contemporary Anglo-Irish novel, its conditioning by "the facts of Irish history and the realities of social and cultural attitudes in Ireland" is crucial. But it is equally crucial to remember that Irish history, social, and cultural attitudes are not developed in a vacuum. Ireland is a participant in world affairs, sharing a post-colonial role with other nations. One arena where this is most obvious and important to both the novel and the nation is the condition of women, especially within the context of the privileging of the nuclear family in Ireland. The Irish family, in its role as ethnic and cultural standard-bearer for the new nation, has been the subject of hundreds of Anglo-Irish novels in the twentieth century alone. And any novel about or study of the family necessarily situates women primarily within it--as mothers, wives, daughters, sisters--and within the heterosexual unions that lead to families--as lovers. Jordan's and McGahern's works are different because they don't merely include women but focus on them, addressing the woman within the family and patriarchal heterosexuality because the authors see women as the key to understanding the nation-building processes of the Republic.

For women, both in Irish society and Anglo-Irish literature, provide the most consistent evidence of fragmentation of the national identity. Thus the condition of women in the socio-politico-literary post-colonial Republic of Ireland is at the heart of this study; first one must examine the Irish women's socio-political identity, then their literary identity.

Typically in post-colonial states, racial and ethnic diversity, the legacy of years of empire, causes unrest within a new state as minority groups--the Armenians in Turkey, the Kurds in Iraq, etcetera--seek self-governance. Crushing these rebellions against the official state leads to human rights violations such as "ethnic cleansing."[10] But Ireland, lacking a real ethnic or racial other in a very homogenous state, created its alien menace in its own "unrestrained" women. Minister for Justice Kevin O'Higgins could justify the Free State's many negative policies concerning women by maintaining that, since it had been an issue while Ireland was governed by Britain, women's equality "was not demanded by the Irish electorate... 'but because we were at that time part and parcel of the political system of Great Britain it applied here [in the Free State]'" (Clancy 1990, 224). Women had been protected by the colonizer--Great Britain--and so after independence were viewed to a certain extent as collaborators; activists for women's rights were seen as serving the interests of the British. In a state where citizenship is based fully on inclusion in the one single ethnic identity recognized by that state (Irish), ethnicity is the only form of political empowerment. Thus Irish women would be doubly alienated--possessing few of the constitutional protection of citizens, yet subject to the harsh obligations of permanent residence in Ireland. Irish women were treated like permanent resident aliens in their own state.[11] But this does not mean that Irish women were powerless in the new Republic. They would manifest a performative resistance to the marginalizing, dichotomizing role assigned to them by the state and reaffirmed in literature. Irish women would offer performative resistance to the essentialism of the new Irish Republic.

"Essence" is part of the preoccupying search for the "nature" of the Irish and all their works, for the truth of that deep natural self as revealed through the thoughts and words and deeds of those men who possess true Irishness. The outline of traditional Irish studies I gave above is an illustration of essentialist criticism. The struggle to define and provide ethnic purity is not a new one, nor is it unique to the Irish. "Performance" is a slightly more difficult term, as it has many possible uses and meanings. In this case, I am using the term "performance" to mean an acknowledgment of the social constraints within which all human actions take place, and which shape all human possibilities. Performance recognizes that agency is limited and reactive; at best a constantly changing response to circumstances which, on the one hand, one cannot dictate but which, on the other hand, one does not merely passively encounter or endure. Performative agency is, then, a compulsory negotiation of events which one simultaneously shapes and is shaped by. This determination by social forces does not disallow resistance, but it does dictate certain specific kinds of resistance. In post-colonial Ireland, de-colonization and new nation-building form the social milieu and thus dictate that social non-conformity means reacting against the essentialism that de-colonized nation-building relies upon. In *Bodies That Matter: On the Discursive Limits of "Sex,"* Judith Butler provides a good working definition of this kind of performance:

> ...I would suggest that performativity cannot be understood outside of a process of iterability, a regularized and constrained repetition of norms. And this repetition is not performed *by* a subject; this repetition is what

enables a subject and constitutes the temporal condition for the subject. This iterability implies that 'performance' is not a singular 'act' or event, but a ritualized production, a ritual reiterated under and through constraint, under and through the force of prohibition and taboo, with the threat of ostracism and even death controlling and compelling the shape of production, but not, I will insist, determining it fully in advance. (her italics--Butler 1993, 95)

Thus, the repetition of nation-building norms of ethnic pride and purity enable the nation's subjects and constitute their temporal conditions. I agree with Butler that not all resistance is predestined to follow this rule. But the resistances to Irishism are determined to a large extent by nation-building to be acts of resistance against xenophobia and naturalization of Irish ethnicity. And, in Ireland's case, resistance against the state means resistance by women (and, ideally, men) against the institutionalized alienation and denigration of female identity. Thus sexuality is built in to the question of ethnicity, and feminine sexuality becomes almost an ethnicity unto itself, denied as it is any positive role in Irish ethnic policy, as I shall show at greater length in Chapter One.

My focus on Irish women's roles in re-making the state is facilitated by a comparative context. By discussing Irish women in relation to Ireland's post-colonial national project, I mean to include Irish women in the long-standing international debate on the necessarily perverse relationship of women to the modern state. By comparing the repressive measures their state has taken against women in Ireland to those their state has taken against women of non-western nations, I neither privilege Irish women's issues nor dismiss them because of their seeming "First World" geographical location. Inclusion is not privilege.

It is within Anglo-Irish literature that my interest in breaking down this dichotomy between male essence and female performance by revealing their discursive relationship can be exercised. Here the literary identity of Irish women comes into play. The pre-modern idea of maintaining a pure Irish "essence" was from the start on a collision course with the reality of the post-modern fracturing of identity, individual and national, and the effect of those collisions on those extolling essential Irish national identity (both within the government and within the literary world) was an effort to ever more sharply define essence as opposed to performance. Therefore most political and literary works are efforts to document unbridgeable difference. McGahern's and Jordan's texts, however, are concerned with revealing the performative nature of essence itself, with showing how the Traditional Irish Identity was as much a staged construct of reality as any "subversive" identities performed by women. Jordan and McGahern view women's position in the Republic as important because it is key to perceiving a discursive rather than a dichotomous relationship between femininized performance and masculinized essence; discourse between the male and female characters breaks down dichotomies between male "essence" and female "performance" until essence is revealed to be as much a performance as any "female" loss of identity in, as Jordan puts it, the "whorls" of the modern world.

Because I want to deal with the concurrent importance to and marginalization of women's struggles within and against post-colonial nationalism in the contemporary Anglo-Irish novel, I have chosen texts which best incorporate and are most basically affected by these issues of insulation and women's resistance. Surprisingly, in this case I found those texts consistently written by two men--John McGahern and Neil Jordan. The flight of female Anglo-Irish novelists from contemporary Ireland as a residence, topic, or site for their novels is, of course, a comment on the hostility of modern Ireland toward its female citizens. Julia O'Faolain serves as a good example of how many female Anglo-Irish novelists have regularly turned from writing about contemporary Irish society; her latest novels have been set in fifth-century Europe, present-day Italy, and California. While this diversity of subject matter may seem unexceptional, for Irish authors it is very unusual, as Ireland remains the strictly all-engrossing, almost inescapable topic of Anglo-Irish writing. This turning away deserves a study in itself; as I want to site my study in contemporary post-colonial Ireland so I can deal with de-colonization effects on women, I chose texts which addressed this issue. That they are male-authored is itself a comment on women's roles in contemporary Ireland, as men are more able to address socio-political issues within the Irish family because they were granted more authority to speak for it. McGahern's and Jordan's texts are all about male and female categorizations and the resistances built in to such strict segregation; they are not comfortable with these issues, and at times they seem struggle against them as they continually crop up as if by relentless accident. But these very factors make

McGahern's and Jordan's texts crucial reading for any study of women's post-colonial issues as rendered in fiction.
I hope to avoid hierarchizing McGahern and Jordan by following three strategies: first, by studying their common themes at once rather than discussing McGahern's works first and then Jordan's, thus lionizing McGahern's chronological head-start and lengthier career; second, because of the filmic nature of his prose fiction, by treating Jordan's screenplays as works of prose fiction. Then, I treat McGahern's and Jordan's works as equally representative of themes of sloughing off institutional Irishness, despite the tendency to view McGahern as the grand old (wise) man of Anglo-Irish letters and Jordan as the uneven upstart. McGahern, an established author, has until recently received much more critical attention than Jordan. Yet both have suffered, in different ways, from Anglo-Irish criticism, with its judgments based on the unreliable criteria of Irishness and "tone" (which I will discuss at greater length below). Evaluating that critical reception, in the form of reviews as well as scholarly articles (which often show very little differentiation from one another) will play a major role in my investigation. But it is the unread texts of each author that I will be focusing on most sharply--the post-colonial texts which address the continuing colonization of Irish women based on fear of the performative nation they both threaten and represent.

Notes

1. Throughout this work I will be dealing exclusively with the literature, culture, and history of southern Ireland, the Republic of Ireland (Eire). "Ireland" is a loose term but it is generally taken as referring to the Republic and not northern Ireland, the political entity still attached to Great Britain. When clarity demands, I use the term Republic; otherwise, it is assumed I am not speaking of northern Ireland, which necessarily has a much different literary-historical context than does the Republic.

2. See the introduction by James Simmons in *Ten Irish Poets: An Anthology of Poems* by George Buchanan, et al, Cheadle Hulme: Carcanet Press, 1974, for an enactment of this inevitable naming predicament.
The accuracy of the term "Anglo-Irish" is disputed. For as long as Irish has been a minority language in Ireland, there has been controversy over what to call works written in English by Irish writers. Several terms are in use at present, including "Anglo-Irish," "Irish-English," "Hiberno-English" and "Irish." I prefer not to refer to works written in English as

"Irish" literature, as there is a healthy body of works currently being written in the Irish language. I refer to literature written in English by Irish authors as "Anglo-Irish;" however, many critics and authors I cite refer to this literature as Irish or even English. For partisan feelings about the term, see Andrew Hadfield. 1992. Anglo-Irish Literature: Definitions and (False) Origins. *The Internationalism of Irish Literature and Drama*. Edited Joseph McMinn. ILS vol. 41. Bucks: Colin Smythe, and Alan Warner. 1981. The Growth of Anglo-Irish Literature. *A Guide to Anglo-Irish Literature*. New York: St. Martin's Press.

The term Anglo-Irish is applied to literature, while the general field of study of literature and political culture in Ireland is still referred to as "Irish studies."

3. Innes' book is instructive because of its exhaustiveness. Most comparative studies of Anglo-Irish literature are in article form. The few examples include: Maureen S. G. Hawkins. 1992. *An Giall, The Hostage, and Kongi's Harvest:* Post-Colonial Irish, Anglo-Irish and Nigerian variations on a Post-modern Theme. *The Internationalism of Irish Literature and Drama*. Edited Joseph McMinn. ILS vol. 41. Bucks: Colin Smythe; J. P. Clark. 1992. The First Doing: A Nigerian Encounter with Irish Literature. *The Internationalism of Irish Literature and Drama*. Edited Joseph McMinn. ILS vol. 41. Bucks: Colin Smythe; and Ruth Fleischmann. 1992. The Insularity of Irish Literature: Cultural Subjugation and the Difficulties of Reconstruction. *The Internationalism of Irish Literature and Drama*. Edited Joseph McMinn. ILS vol. 41. Bucks: Colin Smythe.

4. Patrick Kavanagh often expressed a hatred for "the Irish thing;" see Foster (1987).

5. "For several years after the movement...a debate was waged as to whether we could refer...to 'the Irish novel' at all!" (Foster 1987, xii).

A scientific survey is lacking, but I find that of the 90 scholarly collections on "Irish Literature" available in the Stony Brook University Main Library since 1982, around eighty percent concern poetry or drama rather than prose fiction. See Foster's full introduction for a more detailed if highly speculative examination of possible causes for this bias and its projected effects on Anglo-Irish novel writing.

6. I am referring to Samuel Lover, *Rory O'More: A National Romance*, London: Bentley, n.p. 1837, Sydney Owenson (Lady Morgan), *The Wild Irish Girl: A National Tale*, Hartford: S. Andrus, 1850, and Sean O'Casey, *Autobiographies*, London: Macmillan, 1939.

In the index to *The Irish Novel: A Critical Survey*, James Cahalan (1988) lists 18 Anglo-Irish fiction titles from the nineteenth century which include subtitles referring in some way to Irish politics; four of these use the subtitle "a national romance" or "a national tale."

7. See Terence Brown's introduction to *Ireland's Literature* for more on "the pre-eminence of history among the humanistic disciplines practised in Irish academe" (Brown 1988, vii).

8. Edna Longley provides an especially telling example of the circularity of this logic as evidenced by critical pillar Seamus Deane: "Deane's criticism frequently travels in a loop whereby he first seeks to disprove 'such a thing as an Irish national character or an Irish fate or an Irish destiny' but then reverts to Nationalist language: 'it is indeed true that *we have* in this island, *over a very long time*, produced a literature or a form of writing which is *unique to us*'" (her italics-Longley 1994, 25).

9. "I think it would be true to say that issues like [literary developments since Modernism and interdisciplinary forms of criticism] have never been really prominent among the concerns of Irish writers in this century, nor among those who write about Irish writers...We admire our writers for other qualities...one would scarcely describe [Irish writing and criticism] as a literature possessed of interesting, dynamic ideas about its local society." Thomas Kilroy. 1982. The Irish Writer: Self and Society, 1950-80. *Literature and the Changing Ireland*. Edited Peter Connolly. ILS, vol. 9, Bucks: Colin Smythe, 181-182.

10. The paradox of disregard for human rights in states which fought against colonial oppression and inequality is described by Taheri:

The argument most often used by governments in their attempt to justify the slow progress achieved on human rights is that...economic development [must be] top priority...The assumption that respect for human rights must somehow compromise a nation's economic development is general...The paramount role played by the state in economic decision-making in most countries...[is] often dictated by ideology. The authoritarian model of development [in Iran] was not seriously questioned until the 1970s... The period 1950-1980 was marked by a general fascination with big projects aimed at strengthening the state. (Taheri 1988, 257-258)

11. This attitude led to many acts of legislation whose violence toward women was implicit, such as the refusal to raise the age of consent from 15 to 18 in the case of indecent assault (Criminal Law Amendment Bill, 1935), an amendment "which was described as 'absurd' by [Prime] Minister [Ruttledge]" (Walby 1992, 215).

Chapter One

Engendering the post-colonial

> In the Name of the Most Holy Trinity, from Whom
> is all Authority and to Whom, as our final end,
> all actions both of men and States must be referred,
> We, the people of Eire, Humbly acknowledging
> all our obligations to our Divine Lord, Jesus Christ,
> Who sustained our fathers through centuries of trial
> ...Do hereby adopt, enact and give ourselves to this Constitution.
> --Preamble to the Irish Constitution

> My marriage was arranged by a cousin of mine. He said
> I would be suitable for the slaving! (Beale 1987, 26)
> --Alice, Co. Clare

In order to understand the male-female relations portrayed in McGahern's and Jordan's works, de-colonized Irish society must be properly defined, not only within the larger post-colonial framework it shares with other former colonies, but within its own unique response to the challenges of de-colonization. The state which went from colonial Ireland to the short-lived Poblachta Eireánn (1916) to the Free State (partition) to the Republic of Eire (1949) was a geographical and ideological morass badly in need of a unifying ideology. Because of religious and political factors particular to Ireland, that unifying ideology revolved punitively around women. The brief history of women's positioning in the post-colonial Irish nation which follows should be read not only as necessary background to contemporary Irish politics but as one strand of a de-colonizing experience which has been acted out in many different areas of the globe since the beginning of the century.

The search for the pure, essential Irish discussed above as a result of colonial denigration of Irishness was carried into the politics of post-colonial nation-building in the era of the Free State and the Republic (Eire). It was difficult to resuscitate pure Irishness when the adaptation of English economic systems and planning, along with financial borrowing from England, necessary to building the new nation economically, conflicted with the national ideology of separation from England and complete independence from outside influences in the new, Catholic, Gaelic Irish state. Often the task of the post-colonial nation is to create a new national agenda once the fight for freedom is over, and often that new political agenda is contradictory to the ideological agenda of independence which enabled it. In Ireland's case, the new state had been enabled largely by the efforts of women, yet it developed a national ideology which reduced Irish women practically to slaves.[1]

In post-colonial women's experiences of being called to nation-build, they are generally looked to by male leaders, and women's liberation is very important since it symbolizes the liberation of the country (following the heterosexual colonialism-as-rape-of-a-woman model).[2] Kumari Jayawardena sums up this reciprocal relationship between national and women's rights in non-western nations: "[With] the rise of nationalism in non-European countries, women's emancipation and education became primary issues, both for the women of the bourgeoisie and for male reformers...In several countries of the Third World the question of voting rights for women was posed, especially during heightened phases of the nationalist struggle, when the issues debated included the right to self-government and equality" (Jayawardena 1986, 15-16, 18-19). Jayawardena notes that the status of women during and after the fight for independence in most Middle- and Far-Eastern nations was crucial to the longevity of new regimes. "[Struggles] for women's emancipation were an essential and integral part of national resistance movements. In all these countries [Turkey, Egypt, Iran, India, Sri Lanka, Indonesia, Phillipines, China, Vietnam, Korea and Japan], the 'woman question' forcefully made its appearance during the early 20th century" (Jayawardena 1986, 8). Reforms granting women access to education, the vote, and/or freedom to travel and dress as they liked were implemented in many new nations and, whether successful or rescinded, these reforms were central to nation-building experiments. Women were recognized as an important workforce and charged with raising the future citizens of each nation, and they were well-organized: feminist journals and political organizations flourished in many Middle- and Far-Eastern nations, sometimes through the efforts of male literary/political leaders.[3]

In Ireland, however, women were never turned to willingly as a separate work force by men; rather they were defined strictly as reinforcements, working only to supply their male leaders' basic domestic needs.[4] Although women performed the bulk of the work on the farms comprising Ireland's overwhelmingly rural society, they were not counted as laborers in the census. This imbalance was largely the result of Catholic influence on the Irish people. The woman's only valid role in a traditional Roman Catholic society was Mother, and Ireland was, from its inception in the 1916 Rising at the latest, to be a Roman Catholic nation. Irish leaders clung to Ireland's Catholic heritage as proof of Ireland's status as the first civilized western people--had not Ireland, land of saints and scholars, sent out the missionaries who converted and civilized the rest of Europe, especially England? Ireland's early exposure to Roman civilization as represented by Christianity was to affect its colonial program because, unlike most other nations going through de-colonization, Ireland did not feel the need to adopt western religion, attitude, enlightenment, or cultural history. "This strong national feeling is based upon a consciousness of race, of belonging to a peculiar people descended from the heroes of the Golden Age, the defenders of a great civilization who were the victims of ruthless, foreign invaders who were inferior in everything but force of numbers" (Ayearst 1970, 66). More recently even than Ayearst's book is Thomas Cahill's 1995 volume, tellingly entitled: *How the Irish Saved Civilization: The Untold Story of Ireland's Heroic Role from the Fall of Rome to the Rise of Medieval Europe*. Irish leaders considered their country already a western nation--the first western nation, in fact, and therefore they departed from the usual policy of post-colonial nations which affirmed and hearkened back to ancient, pre-colonial matriarchy or equality for women. Thus the (at least expressed) desire of many non-western male leaders to shake off the misogyny of traditional religions in order to achieve a society based on European humanism had no place in post-colonial Ireland, where male leaders saw the Ibsenian "new woman" and women's emancipation as contrary to the traditional Catholic, western values Ireland had first introduced to the rest of the world.[5]

Another reason for the unpopularity of women's emancipation in Ireland was the involvement of British women in suffrage at the turn of the twentieth century. British suffragists supported Irish women's suffrage in sympathy with Ireland's struggles for Home Rule-

-ironically participating in the symbolic parallel of national and women's struggles for liberty. Unfortunately, the involvement of British men and women suffragists in Ireland was viewed as British political infiltration of the Irish nationalist movement: "One nationalist wrote: 'The suffrage movement is turning thoughts of the average Irishwoman Englandwards. That is its greatest danger in the present state of this country.' On this ground alone Irish politicians felt they could claim that women's suffrage was not an Irish issue and therefore need not be on their political agenda" (Luddy 1990, 182). This attitude, that women were traitors because they sought suffrage, set the stage for official suspicion of women's efforts in the War of Independence and Civil War (1916-1922). Most Irish women were staunch supporters of the Irish Republic (Poblachta Eireánn) announced from the General Post Office in Dublin during Easter Week 1916, and continued to fight against compromising the official declaration of equality for all citizens, male and female, contained in the original 1916 constitution. Cumann na mBan (Irishwomen's Council) was formed in 1914 to organize and mobilize the women's fight for independence, and was gradually co-opted as an auxiliary of the IRA. While the male leaders of the IRA designated Cumann na mBan as merely their domestic providers, in reality the group grew to include thousands of women who ran guns, cared for wounded, hid wanted men and generally formed the backbone of domestic resistance during the War of Independence and the following Civil War. Irish women were anxious to support an Irish state which granted them full rights of citizenship, as the manifesto of the Irish volunteers before the 1916 rising "pledged the organisation to 'secure and maintain the rights and liberties common to all the people of Ireland'; an ambiguity the feminists were determined to clarify because, in legal terms, *a woman was not a person* (person being defined as a male person)" (my italics-Ward 1983, 96-97). The proclaimed Irish Republic promised recognition of women as fully Irish citizens.

So it was their involvement in the Civil War which earned Irish women alienation from the fathers of the nation. The Civil War resulted from division over the Home Rule offer made by the British in 1921 which partitioned the country into two states and created the contested geography of Northern Ireland. The IRA did not accept this treaty on the basis of the partition and the fact that Ireland would remain within the British Commonwealth with the same status as South Africa, Canada, New Zealand and Australia; an oath of loyalty to the British Empire would be required of all those seeking to hold office. Cumann na mBan and other women's groups did not accept the treaty for the same reasons and because it rescinded women's suffrage and denied women full citizenship. The male leaders of the 1916 Rising, some of whom who had more sympathetic ties to the issue of women's emancipation, had been executed, and the most influential survivor of 1916, Eamon de Valera, while opposed to partition, was, due in part to his Catholic beliefs, absolutely opposed to women's emancipation. The other male leaders, especially Arthur Griffith, first president of the Free State, were anxious to seize their chance at even limited independence, and wanted to accept Britain's terms. Therefore, "those who supported the Treaty persisted in condemning the motion [to hold out for women's suffrage] as an opportunistic attempt to jeopardise the Treaty."[6] When the Irishwomen's Franchise League asked Griffith to revise the electoral register so that it reflected women's opinion on the Treaty,

> Griffith's answer was that, first, the Dáil [Irish senate] had no power to alter the franchise, second, that it would take at least eight months to alter the register, and, finally, Britain would refuse to recognise the validity of an election held under terms that differed from those already agreed and consequently the Treaty would be in jeopardy...Kate O'Callaghan...denied her motion was a cynical calculation to discredit the Treaty. It was a proposal, in accordance with the spirit of the [1916] Proclamation, to remedy an injustice to Irishwomen who had fully participated in all the dangers of war...Griffifth angrily dismissed these arguments [as] 'a trick on the Irish people,' devised by those who sought to 'torpedo the Treaty.' (Ward 1983, 174-175)

Women who appeared before the Dáil to protest the terms of the Treaty were accused of mental instability brought on by the horrors of war.[7] The Treaty was accepted, and many women turned their efforts to supporting the IRA in its battle against the new Irish Free State during the bloody guerilla fighting of the Civil War. Irish women in Cumann na mBan stated that they fought for the Irish Republic "where sex was no bar to citizenship...recognition of the Republic [rather than the partitioned Free State] was inextricably linked with recognition of women's right to equality" (Ward 1983, 178).

The Civil War was lost to those who supported the Treaty, and the new Free State government portrayed those who had fought against it, especially women, as traitors to the Irish state. When the

Republic was lost, so was the recognition of "women's right to equality" linked to it, and women's emancipation became officially a dead letter. This set the stage for Irish women to be treated like aliens, and denied full citizenship. The very male organizations which relied on the heroism and commitment of women throughout the wars now erased women's participation in liberation from the official historical record and set about containing the dangerous force of Irish women and their political organizations.[8] Women had never been encouraged to actively participate with men in the struggle for freedom, they had volunteered to do so and often fought for that right. Now, in return for their opposition to the Treaty, women would find themselves written out of full citizenship in the legislation culminating in the 1937 Constitution. Thus, the Free State was marked from its outset by conflict with and opposition from women.

The State Recognizes (a certain) Family

> Fearing the castration of modernity, an "infantile"
> (or early-modern) polity has constructed a fetish
> of its own retarded essence ("our way of doing things")
> and imposed an instinctive taboo around it. (Nairn 1988, 114)

> One woman in the house must always be working.
> --Irish proverb

Coming into statehood on such a weak leg--severe internal social and political upheaval--meant the leaders of the Free State had to create policies to control economics and women quickly in order to restore domestic peace. In a series of legislative moves crowned by the 1937 Constitution, a purgative domestic policy was pursued which aimed at strengthening the economy by strengthening the nuclear, patriarchal family: homosexuality, contraception, abortion and divorce were made constitutionally illegal in order to curb access to single and/or alternative lifestyles.[9] Women were deliberately targeted for containment by this legislation, primarily represented by the desired role of "Mother" it created and enforced.

As mothers, women are denied a political voice, importantly, because even their motherhood is not allowed to leverage any political power. Mothers are honored as fonts of the nation, but underlying it all is a sense that they are basically a threat (hence the ugly mothers in so much Anglo-Irish fiction). This attitude is still current in Ireland, where in 1983 an amendment to keep abortion from ever being legalized by prohibiting a change in the 1937 Constitution was passed. The amendment was supported by an ad campaign which "shows a baby. The mother...is not shown. The woman has been removed. Separation of woman and womb has now been achieved...We have been wiped out. We are the disappeared. We are not to be trusted. Our wombs have been kicked right out of us. No woman can be trusted with a womb of her own" (Beale 1987, 117). Women are described as holding the position of mother not because they want to fulfill their natural duty, but because they are forced to, against their unnatural will. Women by their very nature pose a threat to the state which even their role as mother does not fully overcome. This rigid separation of women from active citizenship reinforced the slave-like status of the women who had no part in "the state of the nation" and whose presence to men was "a disturbance." Molly Mullin points out that recent scholarship has argued that "this sort of patriarchal familialism...is an ideology that developed partly in response to social and economic conditions resulting from British colonization and the nineteenth-century famine;" in this way it follows a predictable colonial pattern (Mullin 1991, 43). While this separation exists in other post-colonial nations, however, its reification in contemporary Irish law is unusually complete and unforgiving.

In *Women in Ireland: Voices of Change* Jenny Beale notes how women's reproduction and restriction to the home became key to Free State economic policy:

> The industrial base of the country was very small and the isolationist policies of successive governments prevented any significant industrial development until the 1960s. Economic policy was based on the idea of national self-sufficiency, relying on farming and indigenous industry. The small farm was the key economic unit, and to support it, the family was the key social unit. To politicians, the family was the basic unit of the rural economy; to the Church it was the basis of Catholic society. The family had such an important function that its role was enshrined in the 1937 constitution:
> Article 41.1.1 The State recognizes the Family as the natural primary and fundamental unit group of Society, and as a moral institution possessing inalienable and imprescriptible rights, antecedent and superior to all positive law.

2. The State, therefore, guarantees to protect the Family in its constitution and authority, as the necessary basis of social order and as indispensable to the welfare of the Nation and State (Beale 1987, 6)

It is difficult to tell from the wording which has constitution and authority--the State or the Family; in practice, it would be shared equally, equating the Family with the State.

Here the key role of female containment in economic growth is plainly assumed. The basis of Free State and, later, Republican, governmentality is its function of keeping women in the home reproducing. In Article 41.2.1, "the State recognizes that by her life within the home, woman [sic] gives to the State a support without which the common good cannot be achieved," and that "the State shall, therefore, endeavour to ensure that mothers shall not be obliged by economic necessity to engage in labour to the neglect of their duties in the home" (Beale 1987, 7). Policy concerning homosexuality, unwed motherhood, divorce and contraception were equally restrictive. One of the more infamous laws was the Marriage Ban, which forbade married women to work outside the home; if a single working woman married she perforce lost her job, and if she lied about her marital status she was subject to fines and legal action. This law was repealed only in 1973, and Ireland's percentage of married working women in 1981 (17.4%), while representing a threefold increase since 1961, is still far below the EEC average of 42% (Beale 1987, 145).

Richard Breen, et al., in Understanding Contemporary Ireland, state that from its beginning the state in Ireland

> adopted a strongly conservative approach to gender roles and family relations...[and] the exercise of the permitted 'moral restriction' on sexuality was strongly influenced by economic selectivities which acted to reduce substantially the marriage chances of the class categories experiencing economic marginalisation...the state's role in shaping the contemporary Irish family...for the most part supported the stability of the conventional family...however, the State's generosity has not extended to financially compensating women for the child-rearing responsibilities so cherished in the Constitution or to equalising the costs of child rearing through redistribution of income. (Breen, et al 1990, 120,199)[10]

What these figures make apparent is the fact that the Irish government's policy on women has created a specific sort of Irish ethnicity based on gender. Women could vote, but many would not, as their needs and demands would be consistently ignored by the government.[11] While seemingly included in and central to the state because of their role as mothers, in fact women were not true citizens of the Irish state, and therefore were not truly or completely Irish. Those who did not conform to the patriarchal family ideology were criminalized and punished, and the State put women in the position of criminals by targeting women's basic reproductive, employment and divorce rights for suppression. The Free State Constitution was so unfair to women it raised fears of Irish alignment with fascism in pre-WWII Europe and in 1937 the Geneva Convention "blacklisted" the Free State specifically because of its general policy toward women (Clancy 1990, 221).[12]

Thus the Free State cemented its policy of creating a stable middle-class economy and containing the dangers of women, who functioned as the non-national other in the otherwise very homogenous Irish population, while all real Irishness resided in men. The series of economic and social reforms undertaken at this time (1922-present), including borrowing from England and engaging in speculation on the EEC market, upset long-held notions of how the cherished future Irish nation should conduct its affairs. As I shall show, these reforms instilled in the Irish a mistrust and dislike of modernity itself. Following Free State protocol, it is unsurprising that this dangerous entity developed a female gender, viscissitudinous and uncertain, while the heroic colonial past was gendered male in its "unified" and ethnically isolated/pure drive for freedom. The feminized modern Irish state, described as merely performative, subject to foreign (British and American) influences and trends of modernity was without a deep-self, an essential truth, because maternity is not so much an internally-generated identity as a vessel for other, male identities (fathers and, hopefully, sons). This feminine entity was cast at odds with the traditional male, essential Irish identity, not only in literary metaphor but in government policy, as seen above. Official Catholic rhetoric concerning the need to keep women pure voiced concern over distinctly modern problems: "The evil one is ever setting his snares...the dance hall, the bad book, the indecent paper, the motion picture, the immodest fashion in female dress" (Beale 1987, 8). Women are most likely to be seduced by the modern, and then, like Eve offering the apple, to pass the disease of the new on to men.

In like manner, throughout the 1950s and 1960s the novelties of modern nationhood (debt, emigration from the countryside to the cities, mass consumerism) and modern society (popular music, divorce, contraception) were looked upon as female scourges on the nation. For example, by 1977, when the first women's health organizations were struggling to establish themselves in Dublin, at least 2,200 Irish women per year were traveling to England for abortions.[13] These women traveling to England for abortions and birth control, for example, were characterized as infiltrating Ireland with moral decay; like spies, they brought foreign dissipation back into the country and encouraged more women to turn traitor. In the 1970s, as battles for positive women's legislation and citizenship began to characterize Irish politics for the first time since 1916, Irish governments were forced to grapple with the negative economic results of their containment policies. The nation was experiencing inflation and unemployment following the economic boom of the 1960s. Women were working perforce to support their families, and beginning to demand recognition of their contributions to both the state economy and the relative stability of Irish society, the results of their continual work outside and inside the home.

The state did not respond by allowing women back into the national fold; rather, an intensification of the battle to preserve the essential male nation against female performances of modern population control and alternative lifestyles took place throughout the 1970s and into the 1980s and 1990s.[14] In addition to the 1983 referendum which prevents abortion from ever being legalized, the Divorce Referendum, which would legalize divorce, was rejected so that divorce was not only illegal but also unconstitutional. "The 1980s will go down in history as a lousy decade for Irishwomen," stated feminist writer Nell McCafferty; "During what have become known as 'the amendment years,' church and state fought for control of our bodies and our destiny. The Catholic Church won handily...the Irish Constitution contains prohibitions against abortion and divorce...The feminist movement was reduced to survival" (Mulvey 1992, 508-509).

Documenting Performance: The Literary Irish Family

In sometimes circuitous ways, this negative situation found its constant expression in literature. Very few Anglo-Irish novelists were openly decrying the contemporary denigration of women; Edna

O'Brien is a notable exception (her Country Girls trilogy was blunt enough in its representation of the dangers of being a woman in Ireland in the 1950s to be banned in Ireland). Those who did address the "women's issue" usually took one of two routes: a deeply psychoanalytical approach which allowed plenty of room for the safeguard of metaphor, as in *Langrishe, Go Down* by Aidan Higgins; or, the historical approach, which left the brunt of women's oppression safely in the colonial past, as in *The Last September*, by Elizabeth Bowen. In Higgins' novel, the three sisters who are the main characters have their failed lives analyzed in ways that parallel the fate of the nation, which safely neutralizes their tales of emotional repression at the hands of men as parables of the death of the Irish Ascendancy. In Bowen's, the young Irish woman protagonist's suffering at the hands of patriarchy seems to be ended for good by her refusal of an inferior suitor--which refusal is itself enabled, it is implied, by the spirit of anti-British rebellion in the Irish countryside where she resides. In both cases, women's lives and difficulties and political marginalization are made metaphors for the progress of the nation in ways which elide the political reality, the political deliberateness of this marginalization. Women are still romantic figures who have the fundamental apolitical (or tangentially political) struggles of the romantic heroine. The nation is the romantic backdrop for the emotional action of women whose only real brush with politics is having soldiers as love interests or finding their Big Houses burned down.[15]

As I shall show in the next chapter, in Jordan's and McGahern's works women are shown to be actively creating political identities within the new state even as they remain seemingly locked into their prescribed domestic roles. Both men write about the revolutionary past in order to uncover the roots of their social situation decades later. Both men find women crucially (if unacknowledgedly) involved in the formation of the Irish state they write about. And both men see their contemporary society and its characters as the inheritors of social roles created in large part by unacknowledged women. They investigate intimate relationships between men and women in order to uncover the political contingency of those relationships. The domestic, the familiar, is crucially involved in nation-building politics. Put in the context of Jordan's and McGahern's novels about the Irish family, women contribute stable male role models to the new state by enabling their men (usually husbands) within the home--by providing them private, domestic roles as fathers, Irish women provide Irish men with the potential to become fathers to the nation, public father-figures. Female performance in this case defines women using the security provided by outward conformity to the domestic female identity (Wife, Mother) to undermine the patriarchal system which desires to cut them off from the public, political sphere. Female performative resistance means making the domestic political by acknowledging the patriarchal nature of the domestic--the family and the household--and then taking this acknowledgment to its logical conclusion: women who run the household partake in patriarchal power, thus undermining the strictly masculine identity of patriarchy. And the women who run the household play a large role in defining the men they send out into public life. In Jordan's and McGahern's works, domestic women usurp patriarchal power positions by making men dependent upon women's definitions of the public male. This is not simply a case of "the woman behind the man," but a process by which women create a safe space for themselves from which they can change the patriarchal nature of society while seeming to conform to its demands. This is female performative resistance.

What I will show is that the obvious consequence of understanding the active, conscious shaping of male identity by women is realizing that masculine "essence" is a male performance of conforming to the standards of male identity set in large part by women. Men perform patriarchy in that they react to consciously iterated, learned behavioral norms--norms learned in part from women and their performances of femininity. Because it is women who must iterate patriarchal norms in order to retain a safe space--the good woman--in which to work societal change, societal change is necessarily slow. Men iterate the norms they are presented with, and these are patriarchal and so oppressive toward women. But as we shall see in the works of Jordan and McGahern as they progress from describing the turn of the century to the present day, Irish women have managed to weaken patriarchy in Ireland, mostly by gaining legal control of the households they were supposed merely to inhabit and serve.

So the family and its household is the major arena in which performance, both deliberate female resistive performance and unconscious or denied male performance, is studied in Jordan's and McGahern's works. Both writers focus on the family as field of their questioning. McGahern writes bitterly of the nuclear family even as he seems to praise it; Jordan often removes it from the realm of reality, either by eliding it as much as possible in his narratives or by giving it a fantastical treatment.[16] In McGahern's and Jordan's works the father figure represents the forces of the supposedly "essential" Irish individual, while the mother figure represents the gradual, if often unrecognized, triumph of performance over "truth."

Notes

1 (Beale 1987, 26, 37-38). For a lengthy study of how harsh conditions sent many Irish women packing to America and England, see Janet Nolan. 1989. *Ourselves Alone: Women's Emigration from Ireland 1885-1920* (Lexington: University Press of Kentucky.

2 Sara Suleri's book *The Rhetoric of English India* (1992) is a valuable antidote to the heterosexual colonialism-as-rape theory, proving persuasively that colonial relations, based on hommo-sociality between native and foreign men, fail to conform to any model in which women serve as objects of male desire.

3 For example, see Beale (1987, 17, 78, 150-154, 218-225), on Indonesia and Korea respectively.

4 Ward (1983, 11, 12). During the fighting of Easter Week 1916, groups of women took turns doing kitchen and laundry work in the basement of the Post Office as the men fought above; the women were almost completely isolated from any information about how the fight was progressing above them.

5 Confucianism was especially vulnerable to accusations of feudal outmodedness in many nations.

6 Ward (1983, 174). Eamon de Valera refused to allow any women at all to engage in resistance during Easter 1916, and, when overruled by members of Cumann na mBan and other men, refused to fight alongside the many women who did take part by running guns and messages and taking turns as snipers.

7 Ward (1983, 166). In this way, women were blamed for their part in the Civil War; i.e., their "derangement" was just desserts for the horrors of a war they had prolonged.

8   One is hard-pressed to find histories of modern Ireland which mention women's contributions to the struggle for nationhood. The omission of the progress made by the Irish Land League under female management after the male organizers were imprisoned is especially striking. See Ward, Chapter One, "The Ladies' Land League, 1881-1882," (1983), Innes (1983), especially Part Two, and Molly Mullin, "Representations of History, Irish Feminism, and the Politics of Difference" (Feminist Studies 17:1, Spring 1991).

9   While homosexuality was legalized in a surprising move in June 1993, the legislation remains controversial, and the strictures against birth control and abortion remain in place.

10   Breen, et al., (1990, 120, 199). Women in Ireland whose husbands have left them are still ineligible for child support unless they prove abandonment and then seek an annulment--both costly legal processes. The amount of child support the State provides those who do prove abandonment (the "Irish Divorce") and annulment is very small and subject to abrupt cut-offs.

11   Women understood this exclusion to be taking place as the government and constitution of Ireland were formed. Seanad (House) Senator Jenny Wyse-Power, for years the sole champion of women's rights in the Oireachtas (Parliament), protested one legislative act restricting women from jury duty because "if this Bill becomes law the civic spirit that is developing in women will be arrested:"
According to the Senator, the civic spirit of women...underwent radical change in recent times [the wars]. Political events in the past fifty years meant it was the case that 'the men who led political movements and carried them in the main to success utilised women in order to achieve their object.' Such activity greatly promoted women's civic spirit and some women 'encouraged...by the way they have been thrust out...to do work they never did before, came gradually into public life and have done social work which is...successful.' The Minister was doing an injustice...'to what is really a necessary asset to every State, the co-operation of its men and women." Walby 1992, 215)

See also Rosemary Cullen Owens' *Smashing Times: A History of the Irishwomens' Suffrage Movement* (1984) for a complete history of the negative relations between male Irish nationalist leaders and Irish suffragist-activists; especially "Seeds of Unrest" and "Irishwomen Unite."

12   Senator Eileen Costello added her voice to Senator Wyse-Power's, stating that "Women...needed to be educated into responsible citizenship,

since 'they have not realised their power as yet'" (Walby 1992, 222). These women recognized that the Free State, in denying women equal rights of citizenship, was denying that Irish women were really Irish. But the majority of the female members of the Oireachtas were relatives of men killed in the Easter 1916 rising, figureheads only who could be counted on to support the government in even the most violent anti-woman legislation. Brigid Redmond was especially complaisant about de Valera's disregard for women's rights legislation.

13 Sweetman (1979, 151). This chapter on contraception and the efforts of Irish-based women's health groups to establish a presence in Irish politics is a powerful indicator of how taboo women's sexuality and reproduction still are in the Republic.

14 See Molly Mullin on the paradoxes of this association of the powerful female with modernity: "The association of gender equality and modernity is, in fact, particularly ironic in Ireland...[as] 'few peoples have as rich, preserved and recorded a tradition of gynocratic myths'" (1991, 41). Her account of how feminist "counterhegemonic representations of Irish history" provoked a backlash against this gynocratic heritage is compelling.

15 Again, I am leaving out a number of writers, Julia O'Faolain among the more famous, who addressed the inequality of women in Irish society. I do not wish to imply that no one was writing about this inequity. But Jordan and McGahern consistently address how women are at once repressed by and representative of the modern Irish state.

16 In John Cronin's 1992 article on McGahern's novel *Amongst Women* in the Irish University Review, McGahern himself bemoans the Irish novelist's lack of bolstering socio-literary tradition and stability: "'Ireland isn't like other places where the novel has flourished, in that it is so structureless. It has no formed society, no tradition of manners. Because of that, the form of the novel or the shape of a sonnet aren't available to an Irish writer in the same way...Here, though, you don't have a proper society. The whole country is made up of families...the family is a kind of half-way house between the individual and society'" (Cronin 1992, 169-170). It is ironic to find McGahern complaining of no tradition of manners in his society; his rural novels are weighted heavily with the traditional manners and customs of his farm families. It seems possible that what he is really dealing with is the lack of precedent for decoding, deconstructing, and revealing the political agenda (political Irishness) of the traditional manners of his society. In this respect, McGahern was indeed in sparse company in the late 1950s.

Chapter Two

Break up the family

> *"As 'The Colleen Bawn'"*: *The Mother Figure*
> Always love your mother.
> *--The Past*

If the father-figures do not consider their purpose of illustrating essential racial identity as performative but literally essential to the truly Irish citizen, the mother-figures more often acknowledge the intrinsically performative nature of family in its role as a naturalizing, nation-building force. While father-figures end up performing against their will, mother-figures set out to perform resistance to the subjection forced upon them as mothers in the patriarchal families of the new state. Female performance is no accident, and it is completely acknowledged by the women in the texts, if not by the men. In Neil Jordan's novel *The Past*, the theatrical careers of Una and her daughter Rene are evidence of the performance of women being more in step with the times and battling the "essence" of the father. In the novel, an unnamed young male narrator is searching the memories of his mother Rene's contemporaries and consulting his own imagination to piece together Rene's story, for she has somehow been erased from his life. This erasure has diminished the narrator's sense of self and personal identity, and, adrift in the modern world, he seeks through the past to find some context for his existence.

Rene's creation, her formation within Una's womb, is immediately established as parallel to the creation of the Irish state.[1] Una and her husband Michael, who conceived Rene after a Gaelic meeting, have gone to the English seacoast for their honeymoon in order to conceal Una's advanced pregnancy from their relatives and friends in Ireland. Michael spends most of his time walking the beaches in the chilly off-season alone, mulling over his mixed emotions about taking part in either the nascent First World War or the obviously impending rebellion back home in Ireland and eventually engaging in a fantastical sexual affair with a young prostitute. Both Una and Michael are politicized Irish patriots: Una is an actress renowned for her set-pieces enacting moments of heroism and pain in Irish colonial history and Michael is an attorney who becomes involved in Republican cases,

> later assuming a full and active role in what would become the I.R.A. Una claimed it was at her behest, Lili [Rene's childhood friend] tells me...His involvement gradually took its own momentum until by 1919 he had donned the cap and trenchcoat that characterised activists in the upper echelons of the guerilla effort. (Jordan 1980, 46)

This explanation, imagined by Michael's and Una's grandson, is important for unraveling the opposing positions occupied by women (performers) and men (essential) in the novel. Una is lengthily described as a bad actress by Lili, the young girl who feared and disliked her, and the narrator accepts Lili's characterization of Una as loud and always playing herself in the end, an overzealous patriot who performs her freizes for Yeats and other Irish Revival leaders and speaks bad Irish too frequently. Michael, on the other hand, is slowly described in bits and pieces, usually by other people, and his own motives for his involvement with Irish nationalism remain cloudy. The narrator defines him as all subtlety--opposed to Una, who is all-too-literally performance. Seeing their child (the narrator's mother) as a symbol of the unborn nation of Ireland, Michael wills the characteristics of his own selfhood onto Rene.

When he visits Rene alone for the last time before he is assassinated, when she is about six, Michael undergoes a lengthy realization of what he sees as the overpowering bond between his daughter and himself while they are riding on the chair-lift above the sea at Bray: "...he stands and holds her, he is overcome, he lifts her to his chest and gasps over and over again the same few words. You are my child, he says, the chair swaying with him standing, and hers...Always, he tells you, love your mother. And you promise you will" (Ibid., 62-63). Michael is killed soon after, and Una takes over Rene's education and future by putting herself and her daughter into the roles of a lifetime--the widow and orphan of the martyred Irish patriot. Michael wants to leave a lasting influence on the nation and his daughter; the basis for his success in these tasks is crucially misunderstood by the narrator, who sees Una as turning Michael's memory into a parody of grieving devotion which will provide her with the key to the doors of Irish high society. The "crassness" of Una's performance of widow is highlighted by the narrator when she and Rene sit for an official mourning photograph: "Una has been tying and untying your [Rene's] bow, placing her hands magisterially round your head, then striding round the room in her black dress. You know how the long wait is eroding the public strength of her grief" (85).

So Michael is introduced by the narrator from the start as the essence opposed to Una's performance because of Michael's self-removal from the world of the theater which Una inhabits to the world of serious nation-building. Yet Jordan's text is constantly deflating the fatherly pretensions to essential being--most obviously when the upper-echelon of Irish politicians are revealed to be most interested in Una's melodramas. Patriotism is the most performance-oriented profession in the book, as evidenced again by the widespread acceptance and approval with which political movers greet both Michael's death and Una's "public grief." Michael's assassination and martyrdom are but the ultimate performance of patriotism, and it is his death which secures him a place in the canon of great actors of Irish liberty. But whose performance is responsible for Michael's career?

It is Una's. Una, accused by the disdainful Lili and other jealous contemporaries of being a bad actress, is really the best performer in the novel. Una's performance of motherhood is wildly different from Michael's melodramatic performance of fatherhood. She treats her pregnancy with no special fanfare, carrying on an irregular, lifestyle which includes staying up all night smoking and laying in bed all day. When the O'Shaughnessys return to Ireland with the four-month-old Rene, it is Una who pulls off the farce that the baby is only one month old by claiming that Rene was premature and by at once elaborating on the difficulties such a birth entailed and forcing peoples' attention away from the suspect baby and back onto herself. Una immediately returns to acting, and is a hit. The narrator pays a great deal of attention to what he depicts as Una's progress from a bad actress who thinks she is a good actress to a bad actress made uncertain by her realization of her lack of talent to a bad actress who accepts her faults and enjoys being a bad actress. This progression is viewed as a movement from falsity to truth:

> The invitations still came to public ceremonies, but she neglected to attend. For she had gained a sense of humour, a certain delight in incongruity...When asked about her late husband she said, 'Yes, Michael,' and gazed towards the west with her old intensity, but realised now that she enjoyed the pose. She came to see, gradually, around her thirty-fifth year, when the only work she could get was in fit-ups touting peasant melodramas round the provinces, that here was a profession and that she belonged to it. She had always mixed political and feigned passion on the stage, been known above all for her 'sincerity,' her 'truth' of performance...She had...become an emblem, intruded her real self into the theatrical field and for almost a decade it had sufficed....[but] she had realised slowly, like a cured invalid learning to use his legs again, the beauty, permanence and humour of the feigned passion...a parody she enjoyed...[which] carried over with gusto into her real life as slowly, slowly, the balance was reversed and where once she had sinfully pushed the real life on to the stage she now extended the rim of the stage to include her boarding-house, her turn of glance in a rural street and all the minutiae of her private life. (113-114)

The difficulty with the narrator's take on his grandmother's acting is that he does not credit Una with always knowing that her acting is non-realistic. For the case is made within the text that Una alone realizes and admits that the most appealing performance of ethnicity and the politics of nation-building is the most melodramatic one. Politicians and patriots and theater-goers alike want to see their ethnic identity lifted to the level of Greek tragedy or Stoic resistance or Wagnerian grandeur, storm and fury. Rather than discovering the tactic late in life, what Una has always done, to great applause, is move that "rim of the stage" out into the general public, into the slums and respectable neighborhoods and government halls, so that everyone can see themselves playing a part in that epic national identity, even as they buy bread, scrub floors or deliver speeches on Home Rule. Indeed, as we see, she can "take credit" for Michael's political involvement, for by becoming his very visible patriot wife as well as his very visible widow, Una is creating Michael's political impact and reality through her performance of a patriotism intimately linked to or "caused by" his own. She makes him into "Michael," the hero who must be invoked with gaze lifted to the West. Were it not for "the public strength of her grief," Michael would fade into the crowded oblivion of Irish martyrs. Because of Una, he becomes a hero, with a street named after him. Without her, Michael would have remained at the level of futilely trying to decide which performance, rebel or patient legislator, he should take up--which is where we first find him, walking the beaches during Una's pregnancy and trying to make up his mind about which role suits him. In this way, Una can take credit for his role in the rising--she thrust him into performance in a way he could never have done for himself. This is evident at the station upon their return from England, when Michael stands awkwardly holding Rene, utterly incapable of carrying off the deception about her birth. Una takes over, and saves the scheme (41).

Because Una has treated the need for performance seriously does not mean that she does not realize she is performing. We must remember that in the passage above it is the narrator speaking, imaginatively deciding what Una's attitude was after middle age decreased her popularity. Therefore, the opinions he expresses are colored by his investment in finding his own personal essential identity. Overcome by the feeling that the performance aspect of life in Ireland has outweighed the "reality" of his existence, he is searching for the weighty "truth" about himself. He removes Una from his range of options, thereby eliding exactly the information he needs to reconcile performance and identity.

Eileen Vance's performance of ethnicity is also important, especially in relation to her husband's inability to attain performance. James Vance, the photographer who takes Una's and Rene's widow-and-orphan picture when Michael dies, has a relationship with his only son Luke which is similar to Michael's relationship to Rene. Vance's wife Eileen is long dead, apparently having died of grief over James' refusal to convert to Catholicism and ensure Luke's religious instruction (101). James' marriage and fatherhood are remarkably similar to Michael's. He too meets his future wife at a Gaelic lesson and "drifts toward marriage...since he can do nothing else" and finds his marriage soon turned from love to duty, "forgetful on his part and cruciform on hers" (101). James also goes through an emotional, epiphanic realization of his paternal bond to Luke, while walking with the boy on the beach:

> [James'] life rose before him, under a garish light. Why, he wondered, why? And the realisation came...He threw both of his arms out toward that blanket of sea so that they jerked in their sockets...He stumbled down the Head again. Luke! he shouted, Luke! He ran to where the [chair-lift] landed but could only see the ghost of his son below him, tiny running town the shallow field...[James] stood there holding the metal pole, the yellow chair swaying above him. (107-108)

James is a Protestant with a guilty conscience over his family's past wealth, although it is now long-gone and he lives in relative poverty with his father and son. He is an artist, taking photos of Dublin and its people and taking pleasure in his futile efforts to capture reality, the "now," on film. His Catholic neighbors are suspicious of him and his camera, and his Protestant acquaintances disdain him. In these ways he is again like Michael, a loner, thoughtful, misunderstood by his wife yet capable of creating out of love alone, and capable of showing great love for his creations, especially his greatest creation--his child.

Again, the awkward, unintended performative nature of James' entire existence is glaringly apparent. An outsider because of his family's past performance of social difference, James now tries to perform correct Catholic Irishness. His life is spent acting out what he believes essential Irishness to be, and he feels that he has achieved a measure of success by creating his son and performing the role of father. The reason his son can, as James sees it, perform a greater Irishness and by doing so redeem his father, is that Luke is the product of a "really" Irish woman--a Catholic Gaelic teacher. Both Michael and James conceive children in relation to the Irish language classes they take, thereby giving form to their desire to live in essential Irishness. Both fathers see their children as performances of themselves--yet performances drawn from their (the fathers') very essences, and thus both fathers attempt to erase the performance aspect they rely upon. By performing Irish fatherhood, they hope to produce children from their essential selves who will then redeem their fathers' incomplete performances of the desired ethnicity.

Like Una, however, Eileen Vance is immediately defined by her capable performance; in her case, her performance of "true" Irishness. It is the memory of his family's defunct delft factory, "a factory of women," which James falls in love with when he sees Eileen teaching the Gaelic classes he goes to in penance for the sin of his Protestant Ascendancy heritage:[2]

Does he fall in love in memory of them, at adult Irish classes...it is the gulf between them that attracts him as much as the person herself. There is chalk-dust in the air, without the billowing texture of the dust of china. But nevertheless, the young teacher's fingers, which he wants, he needs to hold, are coated white. It is love, but always as an afterthought...when he comes to hold her chalk-whitened fingers which smudge his own in turn, his love gains the intensity of all his mental agonies. Her fingers are Irish, Catholic and youthful. (101)

James, then, falls in love with what he wants to be--"fully" Irish, Catholic and young. Her fingers smudge his with chalk, returning to him his own family past and offering him the Irish language represented in chalk on the board. He wants to possess Eileen to make up the lack within himself, to fill the "gulf between them" which marks him as a Protestant interloper in the Catholic struggle--in short, he wants to join in her performance of national identity. When she accepts him, however, she is alienated exactly by the reason James asked her to enter his life: "She doesn't so much age as contract under the pressure of that gulf...he was kind, like all intelligent men, and therefore amazed when she began to weep one day on the...train...This child will be Catholic, she said...Even if you won't" (101). What Eileen realizes is that James is not willing to join her performance of identity after all, but wishes to appropriate her identity by seeing himself as sole creator of their child, in whom others will recognize the characteristics of the father more than those of the mother, and marvel that such a child could really be the child of the mother and not of the father only (88, 114). James' inability to possess either the essential Irishness he should or a capacity to perform Irishness is symbolized by his mediocre picture-taking. He chooses the "right" characters, dirty Catholic street urchins whom he sees as ultimately Irish, yet his pictures are stilted, lifeless, badly realized. James is a bad actor because he tries to perform essence in hopes that it will become natural to him, and therefore he will never attain the Irishness he desires.

The next mother is Rene. When Una dies suddenly, sixteen year-old Rene goes to the Vance home, ostensibly as an Irish tutor for Luke, and stays for progressively longer periods there, her presence displacing Father Beausang, who visited the Protestant James to discuss his pet theory: a mathematical proof of the existence of the Holy Trinity--Father, Son and Holy Spirit working separately but as one. With Una's death her strong presence is erased from Rene's life, and Rene is almost instantly subsumed into the all-male Vance household. Both Vances become her lovers, and Rene becomes pregnant shortly before leaving Dublin on a tour of Ireland with the theatrical troupe she is part of. Luke goes with her as a stage manager, and James joins them outside Gort, a small provincial town in the west. Lili remembers that when James entered the hotel lobby where the troupe was staying, "Luke...jumped up, opened the other glass door to meet him and said with a voice that could have included the whole world, Father, we are pregnant" (206). Rene maintains to all inquirers, including the Vances, that both men are the father of her child.

The narrator's positioning of this threesome is made extremely clear by his constant insertion of Father Beausang's increasingly mystical conversations with the narrator about the Trinity. The role of the woman is brought up obliquely at first, and then made obvious:

> We walked...As we passed the brash, coloured pieta in the courtyard of the church, I stopped him and pointed at her curved plaster mouth. If the Father, I asked him, fathered His own Son and yet the Son was the Father, does that mean the Son fathered Himself?...In other words, I asked, if the Son fathered Himself, did He by that very act create His own Father? He smiled...You are leaving out, he whispered, the third corner of that exquisite triangle: the Holy Spirit. (182)

Thus in this theory, Rene fulfills the passive role of the Holy Spirit, which is ultimately to make a workable relation between the Son who fathered himself and the Father who created the Son--a fair description of the patriarchal creation of the Irish State.

By fostering this reading of his parentage, the son who feels so stripped of essential identity provides himself with a double-dose of the father-figure's essence. Again, the narrator's interpretation of Rene's role as mother is misinformed by his desire for essential substance in the disintegrating modern world of modern Ireland, where, as the narrator tells Lili, "my generation...has forgotten so much" (227). By associating and subordinating Rene to the two Fathers, the narrator hopes to elide Rene's role in his creation or his fathers' lives by making it passive.

But Rene's pregnancy proves her to be her mother's daughter, in that it is an amazing performance that challenges the nature of accepted reality itself. During her pregnancy Rene is onstage nightly as part of a traveling Shakespeare company which is touring the provinces. Yet, although she seems to balloon at four months, she is able to literally hide her pregnancy from the crowds, and spiritually/legally from her companions, by firmly stating that both Vances are the father. Rene is able to convince everyone that this physical impossibility is not impossible, and through the performance of a lifetime she offers the role of father to both Vances. This is crucial; as we have seen in James' case with Eileen, he is incapable of creating and performing a compelling identity for himself. Luke has become a stage manager with the troupe because he has no acting ability. Rene successfully redeems both men by providing them with an identity they can perform--fatherhood. Hence two men constantly described as awkward and apologetic are transformed into the confident and well-loved fathers of Rene's child. This accomplishment rests on the most basic disruption of the patriarchal, nuclear family by denying the authority of legal paternity.

But the narrator cannot accept his mother's transcendent performance, and undoes her gift to his fathers by insisting on trying to figure which man was really his biological father--whose essence does he possess? This in turn problematizes for him not only his mother but all women. The novel ends with a chapter which begins with a line addressed to Father Beausang by the narrator: "Tell me about Woman, I asked him" (230). The perfection of the Trinity, occurring in the thirties, has been exploded by the whorling centripetal forces of modernity which have robbed the narrator-Son of his identity. Lili's characterization of the narrator's birth-day is telling: "It was our last day of course"--she means the last day of the tour, but the meaning reverberates a little further on:

And what, I ask Father Beausang, of woman now? Now as always and his words seem slurred, awaiting the second coming. Can God come twice? I ask and as the road whorls and whorls and we plough through our own clouds he gives me an inventory of signs presaging that event. Son will not know father, he tells me...everything will become everything else. (231)

As the present-day Irish struggle "through their own clouds" son does indeed fail to know his father, and everything merges in a chaotic present. "Woman" especially becomes dangerously impossible to contain and define, as evidenced when the narrator is standing in an empty room and "the scent changed then, as if a woman had entered behind me. I turned, but there was no one there...Then I saw the open window, where the exhaust from the Lisdoonvarna bus was drifting past. Nothing is distinguishable, I realised" (214). The narrator succeeds in undoing the unity of performance bequested to him by his mother and grandmother and recoups instead the uncertain, doomed quest for classification and essence of his fathers and grandfather. Rene, the woman who, as Father Beausang says, "was loved by more than man, [and] could not but give birth to the love-child untouched by time, resplendent, immortal" (230), is reduced to a question mark by her son, who is unenlightened and even depressed by his search for his identity. He ends up tying his own birth to the birth of the Republic under deValera, whom he invokes at his birth-site. The full circle of irony is closed: rather than realize that the nation itself is the child of his grandmother's theatrical performances, and therefore has no essential identity aside from performance, the narrator associates the birth of the Republic with a mystical visitation of a shrine by deValera, "father" of the nation, and assigns de Valera as the essence-bearing Father he ultimately desires most. The freedom of performance is elided and the narrator is sunk back into the hopeless search for essence whose chimerical nature Jordan illustrates.

What both McGahern's and Jordan's texts do is reveal that tension within the family is caused by this division between the masculinized search for "essential" being which denies the feminized realization of resistance to the constructed nature of ethnicity, politics and nationhood. By chronicling the concomitant resistance to performance and the denial of essence which drive the family, they are chronicling Ireland's entrance into the post-colonial era. By locating women within the actual theater, with its obvious definition of performance, Jordan's text makes acting a metaphor for performance. The women's ability to act comes to stand for their ability to resist iterating ethnic norms and to enable men who are not up to snuff politically in the new state: Michael the indecisive dreamer; James the Protestant; Luke the misfit. This female resistance is prescribed, of course, by the social conditions of independence which dominate Irish society at the time, and allow enablements which ironically support the new state: Michael becomes a soldier; James and Luke become valued members of a touring theater praised for its Irish cultural value--all through efforts of resistance against the Irish cultural strictures laid upon them as Woman by Una, Eileen and Rene.

> *"Daddy": The Father Figure*
> "No."
> "No what? No, pig, is it?"
> "No, Daddy."
> *--Amongst Women*

McGahern introduces the Irish farm family by introducing its father. *The Dark* and *Amongst Women* have interchangeable father-figures, Old Mahoney and Moran, and in fact, McGahern's older male characters all partake to some degree of the gruff, rural patriarch. The uncle in *The Pornographer*, the husband in *The Barracks*, the father in *The Leavetaking*, and various characters from the short stories are earlier and later versions of the father first dominant in *The Dark* and obsessively defined in *Amongst Women*.

Old Mahoney and Moran spring from the same source, pre-Free State Ireland. I will focus on Moran in this section rather than on Old Mahoney because Moran is a later, much more complete depiction of the same father-figure Old Mahoney represents; moreover, the qualities which distinguish Moran--his abusiveness and his creation of a household isolated from all influences but his own--are present, if not so fully elaborated, in Old Mahoney. Raising motherless families in the thirties, both characters are caught in the social conflict of the times. Moran is defined by his experience fighting in the Civil War for the nation he now hates. "Look at the country now," he complains to former war buddy James McQuaid; "Run by a crowd of small-minded gangsters out for their own good. It was better if it had never happened" (McGahern 1990, 18). The small farm he now owns is become his whole world because he has willed it so; the household and the family within it take the place of the nation at large which Moran sees as having come into existence at the expense of the laboring poor who brought it into being. When one of his daughters wants to go to medical school, McGahern describes Moran's attitude toward such an institution: "Sheila could not have desired a worse profession. It was the priest and doctor and not the guerrilla fighters who had emerged as the bigwigs in the country Moran had fought for. For his own daughter to lay claim to such a position was an intolerable affront" (Ibid., 88).

This passage is telling, for it reveals Moran's (and Old Mahoney's, who also resists his son's departure for college) fierce separation of the household from the nation. Both fathers believe in their children's intelligence and right to scholarships and other rewards, but both fathers also believe in the inherent crookedness of those offering the rewards, and both fight against their children's involvement with those outsiders represented by professors, priests, professionals and politicians. When McQuaid urges Moran to take his

IRA pension, Moran's refusal is based on typical anti-nationalist grounds:

> 'Many of them who had pensions and medals and jobs later couldn't tell one end of a gun from the other. Many of the men who had actually fought got nothing. An early grave or the emigrant ship. Sometimes I get sick when I see what I fought for.'
> 'It makes no sense your not taking the IRA pension. You earned it. You could still have it in the morning,' McQuaid said.
> 'I'd throw it in their teeth,' Moran clenched and unclenched his hands as he spoke. (15)

Convinced that the Free State is a mercenary unit, Moran withdraws into his own country--his home.

The household is the only political unit McGahern's father-characters recognize, and they themselves are the only arbiters of household politics, dictators who consider themselves benevolent. After experiencing the disappointment of the Free State they fought for, both Moran and Old Mahoney retreated into the rural isolation from which they briefly emerged during the Civil War and closed the doors behind them, sealing off their lives from the life of the state as much as possible. The household is set up as an independent unit, self-sufficient and closed to outsiders, be they Dublin doctors or the family on the next farm. The family they raise is kept as tightly sealed within the house, until the state beckons to them with scholarships and the promise of jobs in Dublin. McGahern's fathers therefore fight a losing battle to preserve their households against the inevitable emigration of their family members. But the very futility of their energies toward preserving the household--the farm, the fields, the stone walls--seems to cause Moran and Old Mahoney to privilege the material entity of home over the family members within it, who are all too prone to desert the stronghold of their fathers.

Thus Mahoney and Moran represent the essential Irishness most appreciated by the state. They are tied to the land, uninterested in outsiders, heads of large families, and veterans of the wars against the colonizer. However, their very seclusion on the farm with their children sets up the performativity of their seeming purity. Moran is very much a performer, constantly striding onto the stage of the family kitchen and overpowering his children, the bit-players, with his stormy portrayal of rugged, unrecognized, under-appreciated mainstay Irish essence. Moran cannot let outsiders into his home because they might turn into hecklers, decrying that his time is past and they must get on with modernization. His children provide a captive, uneducated audience, which can only reflect Moran back onto himself--satisfying, in that Moran can never be questioned, but ultimately unfulfilling because of its limited nature. The children cannot say anything negative about the stifling claustrophobia and isolation of their house for the house is their father himself--he represents the house, the family, the family income and the family *raison d'être*, both literally (he produced the family) and spiritually (he is the epicenter of the family). Moran wished the nation would recognize him; he must settle for his children. Moran ignores this performative nature of his own "essential" being, clinging to and trying to enforce for others his belief in its "truth," and this is what dooms him, for his mid-twentieth century society is being converted to modernity, and his own children will eventually participate in this change and leave home, emptying the theater.

McGahern has Moran think of his family as a larger version of himself many times in *Amongst Women*. His insistence that his children always refer to him as "Daddy" is indicative of his need to possess that all-important title of Father-Creator. One example occurs when Sheila has been forced by Moran to decline her university scholarship:

> Throughout, Moran did not attempt to influence Sheila directly but his withdrawal of support was total.
> After two days Sheila announced truculently, 'I'm not going to the university. I'll take the civil service.'
> 'I don't want to stand in your way, that's why I said nothing, but I can't help thinking it is closer to your measure.'
> 'How?' Her anger brought out his own aggression.
> 'How, what? How, pig, is it?'
> 'What do you mean, Daddy? I didn't understand what you said, that's all,' she was quick to change but she refused to withdraw. (88)

What is revealed here is double: first, that all Moran has to do to influence his daughter is 'withdraw his support,' for Sheila has long been conditioned to require the support of her family (which means Moran, since all the family follow his lead and he is really the whole of the family); second, Moran's insistence that Sheila call him "Daddy" must reinforce for Sheila who and what is making her refuse the scholarship she wants--not some unnamed force of fate, but her father, all-powerful as he is. The scholarship represents the state and its offer to support Moran's daughter in his stead; this rival source of power must be quashed.

This father figure, who spends his life keeping the nation out, maintains that the real nation is not built through politics but through bloodlines and the maintenance of tradition, and in *The Dark* and *Amongst Women* this household work is the work of the family alone. The household of the father is drawn together and desired as a cohesive, holistic unit which battles the fractured nature of modernity. And Moran's or Old Mahoney's efforts are not completely in vain. Thanks to the endless, single-minded labors of the father, most of those children who do go to the city attempt to stave off its decadent wiles by making return trips to the farm to rejuvenate that ineffable sense of self-worth which comes only from their household and their father (who will not leave the house). In fact, all those co-workers of the Morans who also come from the country recognize as honorable the Moran commitment to family which supersedes their commitment to carry out their duties at work. Yet these young city dwellers, though they may respect the rural, isolated families they come from, have nevertheless left them, and even Moran's children will not replicate the family they come from but raise their children in the city as modern consumers.

The motive behind Moran's refusal to parlay with the new state has usually been made out to be honor, integrity and unbending honesty and self-sufficiency. But there is a more intrinsically powerful reason, even more personal than honor or integrity: disorientation. If Moran were willing to kill in the name of independence, even when he was fighting under leaders who he says did not know what they were doing and had neither a real part in the fighting nor the courage to take one, what accounts for this willingness, especially in the face of his later unwillingness to take money from the same leaders he was willing to kill for? The answer lies in the aura of the war as opposed to that of the resulting Free State.

In *Woman and Chinese Modernity* Rey Chow discusses Benjamin's definition of aura in reference to her study of Zheng Henshui's Butterfly novel, *Ping-hu tongche (Beijing-Shanghai Express)*. The confrontation of modernity experienced by the main character in the novel, Hu, devastates him, leaving him ultimately mad. The problem Hu faces is that the gaze he directs toward modern China is not returned with a like gaze which would establish the presence of the new society as well as Hu's relation to it. Instead modern China returns his gaze with "non-reciprocating 'looks,'" as Chow puts it, which refuses to acknowledge the permanence or reality of either Hu or itself (Chow 1991, 79). One can substitute "Moran" for "Hu" in the following passage for a reading of Moran's relationship to the Free State:

> When the proliferation of signs in one's surroundings turns every 'other' into a mass of impenetrable possibilities, how does one know what is 'inside' another, and avoid collapsing into the abyss of the unreturned look? Hu answers by destroying the other's obscurity and molding it into his own shape. The opacity of the modern world is thus accompanied by the individual man's wishful attempt to *forge* a stable perceptual distance from which the unknown others appear to be intelligible...though he never inspires any sympathy for what he does, the ending of the story seems to portray Hu as a kind of mock tragic hero whose downfall is brought about only because he so unswervingly abides by his own 'vision.' In his attempt to 'domesticate' the other, he ends up being left behind. (her italics--Chow 1990, 80)

Moran could justify his involvement in the war of independence and the ensuing Civil War because physical fighting was an object which preserved its aura and returned his gaze. The very dirtiness, danger and remorse of fighting and killing preserved a distance between Moran the soldier and Moran the man; he did what he had to do but never let bloodlust overcome him. He regarded the war as a regrettable yet ultimately comprehensible response to British aggression. Because just war and the honorable soldier have a long tradition in Ireland as in most other cultures, Moran could accept his role in the wars for independence and against partition. He gazed upon an honored tradition and his gaze was returned, for example, by his respectful fellow soldiers, the grateful Irishwomen and men who hid and protected and praised him when he was on the run from the Black and Tans, and by the fear and grudging respect from the British themselves when they recognized Moran's military genius. Fighting was part of the essential ethnic identity.

However, the Free State, being the herald of modernization, did not preserve an aura which could return the respectful gaze. For the creation of the Free State was exactly what signaled the end of the long colonial tradition Moran grew up within. Now the only just war was against poor economic performance, and all the romance of

Catholicism, the common man and Poor Ireland "herself" were part of the campaign to create a large middle class and concern it with getting and spending--ethnic identity changed. The new state returned Moran's hopeful gaze with a "non-reciprocating look," and Moran's response was to withdraw so that he might re-create the mutually respectful aura between the common man and a unity which he could wholeheartedly serve and be recognized by/within. The household fit this description, in that Moran could be recognized within the home by his family members and he could actually be recognized by the household, in that his work there would outlive him in the form of fields he cleared, stone walls he erected, and the modest yet respectable house he left behind. He could make a mark on this "nation" of the household, it would return his gaze with its material bounty while his intimidated children would hasten to establish his performance as the only valid one, and, in fact, accept his performance in lieu of their own, as he dominates the entire stage of their world.

When Moran's efforts to exclude himself from the state which ignored his gaze are looked at in this light, his ultimate failure to create a different state which would acknowledge him alone is anything but a heroic failing. It is, rather, the insistence of one man that he be acknowledged above anyone else, and his willingness to use force on his family members to obtain that acknowledgment even after they may have left his home is comparable to his willingness to kill for independence. His methodical, repetitive cycle of work and rage, so often praised by critics for its rustic "truth," takes on a more cynical implication: "the experience of fragmentation...intensifies the...obsession with, the 'right' details...the adherence to familiar methods and perspectives...A chauvinistic character like Hu [Moran] is shown to be caught by his own interpretation of the world as much by the other's premeditated plot to trap him. This 'other' is not only foreign but also feminine and criminal."[3]

I posit that it is not McGahern's desire to elide this reading of Moran in favor of a heroic, positive one; McGahern positions Moran firmly within the mock heroic, as is evidenced by his deathbed scene. The family has gathered around his bed to tell the Holy Rosary with which Moran has invested such importance and solemnity that it seems to become a part of Moran himself, a performance of Moran, and the family are choking with emotion as they try to imagine life without him. However, Luke, the eldest son who ran away to London, is not present. During the Rosary, Moran suddenly summons his energies to tell his family to shut up; they are shocked, and refuse to stop the Rosary, confused yet trained to let nothing interrupt their telling of the Mysteries. Moran dies (McGahern 1990, 180). That Moran's impending departure from the earth is not enough to bring his disaffected son back home reveals to Moran the futility of his lifetime efforts to force a world into existence which is based on his performance of himself-as-essential. His death is just the final curtain on this performance, and not the end of an era. The mock tragedy of his life's work of enforcing respect is revealed by a scene in the village post office:

> 'How is Mr Moran nowadays?' a customer asked slyly as soon as he [Moran] left.
> 'Not well. He was never well but he was always good at taking care of himself, God bless him,' Annie held her head low over the book of stamps until the ripple of appreciative laughter died. 'They say there wasn't a thing wrong with him when their place flooded last week but he hadn't time to think about himself for two whole days.'
> The burst of laughter was so carelessly dismissive that it seemed to destroy at once an idea that Moran had tried to impose with ferocious will all his life. (173)

This dismissal is what enrages those critics who set Moran up as a tragic hero; McGahern allows it, I believe, exactly because it reveals the ridiculous nature of Moran's agenda. He is perhaps heroic in his dedication to his essential being, yet his time is passed, and so he is forced into ridiculous extremes to try and cling onto his fast-fading existence. His cruelty is not heroic, yet Moran is not a fool. Moran himself has moments of realization, such as the one noted above, during which he accepts his own inevitable marginalization as well as the folly of his violence toward his family. And it is these moments of revelation, combined with the uncomprehending reactions of the Moran children's husbands and wives to the father-in-law they meet at Great Meadow, which recuperate the novel for the reader who cannot see Moran as a hero, nor render a positive reading of his abusiveness. McGahern creates this problematic father to undermine the "essential" aspect of ethnicity, and uses Moran's war experience and his desire to be recognized by the nation to illustrate just how socially constructed his "essential" ethnic identity is.

The Critical Household

In Irish criticism, academic and popular alike, these gender-specific roles are often moralized rather than unpacked. The past, represented by the father, is essential, providing a pure and holistic identity; the present (and, by extension, the future), represented by the mother, is performative, reliant upon "false" representation rather than "actual" being/identity, Thus the fear modernity inspires is a fear of femininity based on an association of the "feminine" with hysteria, fragmentation and the rejection of the essential in favor of performance. The feminized modern Irish nation must then be restored to vitality, in part by the national literature. This critical agenda has prevented readings which validate performance, and therefore prevented positive readings of female characters while encouraging positive readings of male characters. The tyranny of such fathers as Moran is lauded as strength of essential character in the face of those who perform modernity.

Fintan O'Toole's appreciation of *Amongst Women* is an appreciation of Moran; he is the central, single character of importance. O'Toole uses literature as a litmus test of nationhood. He states that:

> serious Irish fiction has all been ironic, playful, the narrator undermining the narrative, reflecting on it, reminding you that this is only a fiction, bouncing from point to counterpoint. Contradiction, parody, multiple points of view, pyrotechnic switches in time-frames, have been all. And for very good reasons: Ireland is like that now.[4]

O'Toole's praise for McGahern's ability to avoid this typically Irish sort of narrative is telling: "So how did McGahern manage to...create this single beautiful narrative that has no interest in contradicting itself, that commands and expects to command the trust of the reader, and that is yet never ever false to this place, that is completely convincing as a story of modern Ireland?"(O'Toole September 1990, 5). O'Toole sets up a powerful paradox: the best Irish literature is that which does not accurately reflect Ireland's current societal upheavals. Looking at the introduction of "The family as an independent republic," we gather that the natural Irish world of the countryside is ultimately appealing to O'Toole, as he describes the fuschia, berries and trees around McGahern's Leitrim home in exuberant, celebratory detail. He also displays interest in and respect for McGahern's humble, rural, family origins.[5] It seems safe to assume that the "real" Ireland for O'Toole is the natural, rural, physical reality of Ireland, unsullied by the industry or human crowds of modernity. This is, of course, the traditional definition of the true Irish state expressed in Eamon de Valera's infamous vision of Ireland as a land of happy, healthy peasants "dancing at the crossroads."

Now we can locate the negativity inherent in O'Toole's definition of "Ireland today." The "contradiction," "multiple points of view," and other forms of chaos which signify "Ireland now" are obviously a departure from the true path of the nation. This is what encourages him about McGahern's novel--it goes back in time to reveal the true nature of Irish society through Moran's essential being, and it can be supposed that perhaps the novel can even help restore that real Irish character by example. This is how a novel which is non-representative of current Irish chaos can be the most truly Irish literature: the novel must be ethnically pure, reflecting and promoting celtic "values" and images, whether celticism is a reality for most Irish or not.

So the Irish nation has a split-personality for O'Toole: it is, in reality, modern and chaotic and decentered; yet, essentially, it is rural and cohesive and holistic. McGahern's novel provides a guide, then, back to the essential Irish self; its literary and social values are thus one. The great merit of *Amongst Women* is its re-discovery and re-validation of the original Irish self, personified by Moran who, as befits a mystical figure, is never shorn of his essential mystery. His "motives," as O'Toole puts it, are never revealed. He is what he is, and it is only through the motions of his daily life that his nature is revealed. This is what makes the "persistence" of Moran's character ultimately fascinating and laudatory--the unfailing nature revealed by his unchanging routine is that of Ireland itself. Hence, Moran the hero. (O'Toole is not alone in following this formula--Paolo Vivante, in "McGahern and the Homeric Moment," praises McGahern's sparse style, comparing the "lack of adventicious information" in his writing to the ancient epic's focus on "uninterpreted" nature/man, thus turning McGahern's protagonists into immediate, classical heros). That given, we can complicate critical espousal of the rural as opposed to the urban by exposing O'Toole's opposition to the "chaos" of modern Ireland as rooted in the sex-dichotomization of pre-modernity and modernity discussed above. Here Chow's description of the critical opposition to Butterfly texts in China in terms of feminization is apt:

Once the interpretive focus is shifted to women, the criticisms that are traditionally made...become...problematic...the charge that...literature is mere 'entertainment,' and that its authors were passive and lazy, pandering to the low tastes of the public. Why are such qualities objectionable? What general cultural associations do they conjure up? A departure from serious nationalistic concerns, an indulgence in the subjective and physical aspects of life, and in improper and immoral modes of behavior? Pretty soon a cluster of discourses that surround the denigrated aspects of feminine sexuality and emotionality, and that conflate the authors with their narratives, emerge in the powerful denunciations of this popular literature (Chow 1991, 51).

Critical appreciation of a novel which can avoid representing the chaos, irony and "subjective and physical aspects of life" obviously finds a sex-based definition. When O'Toole conjures up the image of modern Ireland using these terms, and then lauds McGahern for steering clear of these pitfalls and writing a narrative that "has no interest in contradicting itself, that commands and expects to command the trust of the reader," the feminization of modern Ireland and the masculinization of the essence-bearing father in McGahern's text are starkly apparent.

John Cronin's article, "John McGahern's *Amongst Women*: Retrenchment and Renewal" is an echo of O'Toole's, both ideologically and literally, as he quotes O'Toole's "Both completely Irish and universal" at length as a means of setting up his arguments, which are that the Irish nation is indeed dangerously feminized and that Moran, as representative of male essence, is heroic. Cronin quotes McGahern's identification of "inner formality or calm" as the most important element of a finished piece of writing and approves this idea, stating that *Amongst Women* "finely achieves this necessary quietude" (Cronin 1992, 169). Any novel which reflects modern disunity, commotion or lack of calm is "damaged," and the term "master narrative" takes on new meaning as Cronin begins an appreciation of Moran based on Moran's ability to force a family center into being around himself and his household. Thus Cronin, like O'Toole, begins his critique in Moran's shoes, affirming as natural and therefore laudatory Moran's problematic behaviors.

Cronin's fear of mixing masculine and feminine is revealed by his distaste bordering on outright fear concerning sexuality, which he seems to see as disruptive of male unity:

Innocence and experience, mother love and sexual love, jostle each other uneasily in *The Pornographer* and in...*The Leavetaking*. The signal achievement of *Amongst Women* is its firm avoidance of these mutually irreconcilable disparates... This is a stylistically seamless work, devoid of any lapses into crudity or grossness in its treatment of sex...Moran celebrates his nuptial day by going outside to fell some ash trees, and, when he and his new bride later retire to bed, the bedroom door remains closed and the newly-weds' first love-making is refracted for us...when Moran and Rose have their first quarrel...they soon make up but, again, there is no lapse into crudity or sexual fumblings (Cronin 1992, 173-174).

Cronin's identification of sex as a man's dangerous contact with women (mother love, a new bride) stands parallel to his identification of modern disunity as a dangerous contact for the masculine household.[6]

In Julian Gitzen's article "Wheels Along the Shannon: The Fiction of John McGahern," Gitzen follows critical suit by reading Moran's rages as evidence of fatherly virtue:

Moran's moody and egocentric temperament assures that his family life will have its full share of emotional scenes, all the more so because Moran prizes the family so highly...he is temperamentally unable to...play a part in public affairs...Most of his attention necessarily falls upon 'himself and that larger self of family which had been thrown together by marriage or accident'...To him, 'families were what mattered, more particularly that larger version of himself--his family' (Gitzen 1991, 42).

Gitzen's reading is interesting in its somewhat biological take on Moran's "temperament," especially in relation to Moran's ability to mix with the community at large. McGahern goes out of his way to locate Moran's unwillingness to "mix" within the desire to keep the household separate from the rest of the world, to the detriment of all concerned within Moran's household. But Gitzen reads this resistance almost biologically--it is a result of temperament, supposedly an attribute one is born with--making it evidence of Moran's essence, which is opposed to the outside world and the present.

The number of critical articles on *The Past* is negligible; although Jordan won a literary award for *The Past*, scholarly attention to his work has been limited to short paragraph fragments such as this from James Cahalan's *The Irish Novel: A Critical History*:

> *The Past* (1980) examines fairly traditional materials--the story of characters living through the days of the Abbey Theatre and the birth of the Irish Republic--but in a thoroughly nontraditional way. The narrator presents his fantasies about the lives of his ancestors, moving from confusion to hypothesis to doubt, finally implying that he can be sure of neither who his father is nor who he himself is. He can look at the photographs and other emblems of past but never clearly solve them...Jordan constantly plays with style, point of view, identity, and sexual convention (Cahalan 1989, 301-302).

Cahalan's book devotes five consecutive pages to McGahern and introduces him into other studies a dozen times. Yet I think the reason for Jordan's slighting treatment is the same impetus behind McGahern's popularity: social roles viewed as "fairly traditional materials." McGahern and Jordan are both viewed as describing Irish society in their novels, but McGahern, beginning his career first, has covered it; therefore, though sporadically gifted, Jordan's works are re-treads of situations already well nailed-down. This assumption of the general structure and purpose of "family history" stories like *The Past* leads to much less attentive readings than are warranted. Cahalan's description of the book as the narrator's search for his father completely elides Rene from the novel in its desire to read essential power into the question of the Father and Son components of the Trinity.

Here Cahalan is in the multitudinous company of many scholars and reviewers who, on picking up an Irish novel, insistently read its Irishness--again, asking "Is this book correctly representative of Irishness and how?" rather than perhaps "What is this book revealing about Irishness as post-colonial, gendered performance?"[7] The family is not problematized because it is accepted as a natural site, and any tensions within the family are explained sociologically--as the "natural" conflicts which arise between siblings and parents. Few critics ask, "How does the demand for Irishness itself frustrate the families which are supposed to represent it?" Or, "How is the repression of the female nation at work in the widower household?" Thus the sex-stereotyping involved in the dichotomy between Irish essence and Irish performance goes unread, ironically accomplishing the naturalization of the construct of racial purity which is so irretrievably problematic. The critical response to new readings and performances of ethnicity has been to overlook de-colonization and remain locked into patriotic, colonial needs for and definitions of ethnicity.

Notes

1. Especially Chapter Four.

2. The "Protestant Ascendancy" were the originally aristocratic, landowning, peasant-holding, Big House-living ruling class in colonial Ireland, from whence most known poets, politicians, and other societal figures were drawn. By the final decade of the nineteenth century, land reform had fundamentally weakened their power and fortunes; as their actual power diminished, many of the Ascendancy's members fostered a belief in their intellectual and spiritual superiority to the Catholic masses. The rising in 1916 effectively destroyed this class, though they live on in endless numbers of "Big House" novels.

3. Chow, 79. Chow's book *Woman and Chinese Modernity* is a fascinating study of female performance as represented in literature questioned and stigmatized by a male critical establishment deeply invested in the new Chinese state. The parallels to Ireland are striking.

4. See O'Toole 1990 (September), 5. O'Toole's brand of emotionally-charged, nationalist newspaper literary commentary is apparently popular amongst professional reviewers and scholarly critics alike; see note 9 below.

5. See O'Toole, "The family as an independent republic." (October 1990).

6. In this chapter I have not discussed the character Rose, who enters the Moran household as the second wife, because I want to focus on the widower household dominated by the father which is the focus of the first part of *Amongst Women*. Because of her particular effect upon and importance to that household, I will discuss Rose separately in Chapter Four.

7. The effect of an author's Irish background on reviewers is, apparently, gigantic, overriding all other aesthetic concerns or considerations. Almost all reviewers seem compelled to attribute an Irish author's success or failure in writing on her/his very Irishness. John Mellors' mostly negative review of *The Past* blames Jordan's "marred" work on his seeming "determination that his first novel should win him a place in the Irish literary pantheon" (Mellors 1978, 623). A reviewer of McGahern's *The*

Pornographer claims that "its tone of voice is unmistakably Irish," without explaining what characteristics of the narrative lead to this conclusion-- indeed, it is foregone that the voice of the pornographer must be Irish since McGahern is Irish (Anonymous 1979, 39). Yet the definition of an "Irish tone of voice" remains unqualified. Michael Irwin states that McGahern "has the Irish gift of being able to move fluently and unselfconsciously between a simple and a heightened style" (Irwin 1978, 663). Anthony Thwaite finds McGahern's "intensity and seriousness are of a particularly Irish kind" (Thwaite 1979, 23), while Mary Hope claimes McGahern's prose "weaves and sings as only Irish prose can" (Hope 1978, 25). Bruce Cook, in a review of several books including McGahern's *The Leavetaking*, entitled "The Irish: Pugnacious, powerless, and bored," opens his thoughts on the novel by recalling how his Irish father did not like to be called Irish because all Irish were brawlers:

> While...not the whole truth, it [is] part of it. The Irish are a troublesome race, and no mistake. You have only to turn on your tv set and get the latest news from Belfast to be reminded of it. And should you think the trouble the Irish cause themselves and others is restricted only to the seven [sic-- there are six] counties to the north, then here's a book about them, simply called The Irish to inform you otherwise (Cook 1975, 21).

Once McGahern, and thus his book, are firmly identified by a negative racial background, Cook can go on to describe *The Leavetaking*'s plot at repetitive: "This was the stuff of his first two novels...now we must suffer again with the [mother] through her cancer. We must again endure the meanness of the father...[the dilemma of the main character] is one so characteristic of the ancient hypocrisy in modern Ireland as to seem almost allegorical" (Ibid., 21). These reviews--certainly not alone in their tactics--reveal the perils of racial typing to be, as usual, distorting, and, as usual, especially prevalent when Irish works and writers are under discussion. Unfortunately, this sort of racial typing is usually welcomed by Irish critics as a recognition of the special heritage of Irish culture (see my Introduction for a partial explanation of this phenomenon).

Chapter Three

Courting Performance—Coercion and Compromise

The reliance--whether unconscious or not--of supposedly essential, self-reliant and self-defined men upon the domestic performances of women is investigated before its consecration within marriage by McGahern's novel *The Pornographer* and Neil Jordan's film *The Miracle*. In the former, the protagonist reveals through his profession and his sexual life the pornographic aspects of men's exploitation of women's domesticity, while in the latter Jordan's female protagonist tries to educate her young son to avoid exploiting female performance by entering into a discursive, active relationship with it. Both *The Pornographer* and *The Miracle* focus on the need for men to acknowledge the performativity and, consequentially, the political shaping of the most intimate and domestic roles--lover, husband, wife, mother, father. These texts disallow the exploitation of women by men by invalidating the usual excuses for such male self-centeredness: that the male characters are old, set in their ways, basically decent, gruff yet kind-hearted, and so on. In devaluing these characteristics, each author is powerfully devaluing definitions of traditional Irish manhood and establishing a new, positive evaluation of Irish womanhood.

In *The Miracle*, yet another motherless family is seen through the experience of a young boy.[1] Living with his "widowed" father Sam, Jimmy "James" Coleman spends his days with his friend Rose, making up fantasy pasts and futures for the tourists and locals they see on the beaches at Bray. Jimmy's main conflict with his father is over music; Sam is a saxophonist who plays with the local big band in Bray, and his greatest desire is that his son follow in his footsteps. Jimmy, however, though interested in music, resists, determined vaguely to forge an existence separate from his father's.

In both *The Miracle* and "Night in Tunisia," the Jordan short story it is based on, that individuation comes through contact with a forbidden woman: the local girl-gone-wrong in "Night in Tunisia;" and Renee Baker, an American actress starring in the Dublin production of "Destry Rides Again," in *The Miracle*. Jordan's switch to a mother-figure for the movie is interesting, offering two diametrically-opposed recuperations to Jimmy and his father where the story offered the father nothing but the bitter realization of old age. Alcoholic Sam, knowing the identity of Renee Baker (she is the long-gone wife whom he has told Jimmy is dead), resents her reappearance in his life, as he has made a career of living in the past and her presence reminds him that he has no life at present. Jimmy, on the other hand, sees Renee as his ticket-of-leave from his position of child-caretaker in his father's boozy household; namely, because a sexual relationship with Renee will transform him into a man. As in *The Past*, both men need the female performance to give their lives both a future and a meaning. But the desired performance, of course, varies greatly between father--carefully-preserved memory--and son--sexual adventure/initiation.

Both father and son, then, struggle with what they perceive to be their male essence. Sam's music is his essence, and he cannot do anything else but continue to play the old songs of his youth, though the demand for his big-band music is dwindling in the face of rock-and-roll. On one level, Sam's attachment to the music of the thirties and forties has to do with preserving his legacy; he wants to pass the torch by having Jimmy accompany him with his band at the dance-hall, where he can be introduced and publicly acknowledged as Sam's son, a chip off the old block. But on another level, Sam's desperate refusal to move into the musical present is based on his refusal to let go of his Family Era--when his wife was with him.

Again, the woman of the house is crucially necessary to the male's ability to function, to fulfill his essential needs. When his wife left him with the infant Jimmy, she certainly left Sam's performance of life hanging while she did something else; since she left, Sam hasn't tried very hard to perform as parent for Jimmy, as he relegated that to Renee. Since he has been on his own, Sam has only performed for himself, constantly re-affirming his public self-image, which comes from being the spot-lit soloist in the band. Sam has willed his personal life's performance to stop, taking refuge in music, pulling the curtain on any progression of his interests or abilities away from those in his past. He is like the elephant Rose describes at the circus, who remembers so much the weight of the memories crushes the life out of him. The essence of that remembered past is defined by its music, and by the other band members, with whom Sam drinks late into each night, talking about the old days and forgetting briefly about the new, which are defined in part by Jimmy's disdain for his father's lifestyle.

In this way, Sam is different from Moran, who experiences only brief, unconnected realizations of the fact that his role as Father of the House is indeed a role like any other, dependent upon an appreciative audience and cooperative co-stars within the family and the village. Moran's realizations are so negative that the final one, on his deathbed, helps to end his life. For Sam, however, each day is characterized by the same realization of loss over and over; each nightly performance with his band (a surrogate family/audience) is a reminder of the failure of his performance of Family Man and Husband from which the only escape is drunkenness. But while Sam is actually playing, he briefly regains power over his own literal performance and becomes a Musician whose work is appreciated. Sam's saxophone is for him as Moran's farm is to Moran--the one physical proof of his existence and dedication which will outlive him and thus grant him a measure of immortality.

Jimmy is the unappreciative if loving audience for Sam's retrospective monologues and drunken spiels; like the children in *Amongst Women*, Jimmy is forced to support his father's withdrawal from society, but unlike them (except perhaps for Luke Moran), Jimmy is not in awe of his father. He makes him breakfast, cleans him up, cleans up after him, helps stagger him home, and in general tries to ignore the wifely nature of his caretaking duties to his father. When, in the course of trying to get Sam to leave the bar and return home Jimmy pushes him off balance and Sam falls to the ground, Sam demands an apology in the name of the institution of fatherhood. Jimmy sees fatherhood itself as the gross abuse--Sam's inferior performance of that essential role has soured him on the influence of parents. When his friend Rose's father tells him he blames Jimmy's disgraceful character on Sam, Jimmy agrees. Jimmy also has an audience he depends upon--Rose, with whom he spends his days making up fictional lives and desires for the prosaic people of Bray.

Rose and Jimmy enter the story walking along the boardwalk at Bray, making up a story for an elderly couple--she will acknowledge him as he passes behind her, and they will fall in love. She doesn't turn, but Rose narrates a longing to. Jimmy describes a lonely man in a chip shop as fascinating in his very drabness. They write these choice lines down in Rose's notebook, and continue to speak in the clichés and considered language of fiction, letting the demands of romantic storytelling be their guidelines for expressing emotion and motives--both their own, and those of others. In this way they foreshorten their own agency within their strictly literary "performances." Romantic love is a completely literary performance, and it satisfies their need for diversion, not for giving of themselves. Jimmy and Rose are not yet engaged in performing the roles of the passionate lovers they mouth through their fictions--more than friends, less than lovers, in a strange state of suspended animation, as Rose sees it.

Jimmy is aware of the constructed, staged nature of sexual being, which he sees as a variety of behaviors--Don Juanism, blustering, pining, secretly surveilling, passionately declaring need. Rose, for her part, is toying with the same role-playing, but unlike Jimmy she recognizes that bringing their wordplay into actual performance is inevitable, that acting out, again, is but a metaphor for performance. She decides to take it upon herself to shape a violent clunk named Jonner who has come to town with the circus into a desirable lover while she goes back and forth between performing her pragmatic, non-romantic self and performing a conventionally-desirable and desiring young woman. Rose is aware of the dangers the entrance into performance entails, reminding Jimmy of the need to be kind to one's creations. Jimmy's indifference to her experimental initiation into performance indicates his lack of understanding of it and his refusal to abandon "himself" for a performance of himself.

Renee's enters this world much like an experienced performer who could serve as Rose's mentor.[2] She is Sam's deserter wife, traveling each day on the train from Dublin to Bray to recapture some of her past life there. She is aware of Sam's and Jimmy's presence in Bray, but, treating them more as the characters of her imagination than as real people she might encounter, Renee hazards her daily journey and risks abusing them by her sudden return. Jordan does not make clear her reasons for fleeing her roles of wife and mother, but her fond memories of, yet firm reluctance to face, Sam intimate that she is happier having her performances recognized as such; the burden of performing the "natural" (mother and wife) as a matter of course is too great. Constantly reiterating herself as an actress, she strives to avoid any appeals to essence--thus her refusal to meet with Sam, or to reveal her maternity to Jimmy. She accepts performing in "Destry," but not in the family. This way, her only burden is to an audience which understands that she is not and cannot be who she seems to be. On-stage, a bad performance can be forgotten by its emendation the next night; in the home, bad performance haunts from year to year and manifests itself in a failing family. Thus Renee's tentative willingness to let Jimmy involve himself in her life leaves her sorry for allowing it, for he immediately tries to engage her in the one performance she cannot share with him, and the irony is that Renee is forced to act out the role of Mother fifteen years after she successfully let that curtain drop.

But the consequences of trying to reprise, if briefly, that role of mother are made apparent when Sam goes to Renee to ask her not to tell Jimmy who she is. The setting is telling: Sam interrupts her during rehearsals in Dublin. Previously, she has apologized to the stage manager for being late, and his angry reply that they're all getting used to it makes clear first that her performance is key to the show, to creating its 'reality,' and then that she is negligent in her duty to perform, to give the other performers their *raison d'être*. In this way she is a distinct, if less mystical, echo of Rene O'Shaugnessy in *The Past*; the actress who sustains all those around her through her life-giving performance. All the time Renee and Sam are speaking, the performers are seen in the background, out of focus, waiting on Renee to return so they can continue their act. They are dependent on her, she's the star; without her, they are distant, and unfocused, like her family. In their family roles, Renee as the mother is the star to her family, while Sam the father plays a one-man show to himself alone. In fact, Renee refers to both Sam and Jimmy in separate instances as her "public," which indeed they once were, albeit not the most enthusiastic.

While they are arguing over whether she should reveal her identity to Jimmy, the scene cuts to Jimmy above and beyond them, in the balcony, watching; now Renee becomes fuzzy and indistinct while Jimmy is thrown into sharp focus. When Jimmy visits her afterward in her dressing room, Renee is seated at her lighted makeup mirror, wearing her stage makeup, which heightens her identity as a performer; it is like Jimmy is talking to a star rather than a person. When Jimmy confronts her, she tries to remove Sam to his performance self, The Musician, as well, by stating that Sam was just a musician and that she has known a lot of musicians in her time.

Sam and Jimmy, her family, are the show she walked out on before its run was over, and as a result the show folded; Renee tries to blur the sharpness of her regret by distancing the players. Jordan signals this checkmate and Renee's lack of any easy way out of the return to this threesome--herself, Sam and Jimmy--by holding a long shot on the sign over the stage of "Destry" that says "Welcome to Bottleneck."

Renee knows she should look no further into Jimmy's life, because indeed she does not know him or his father any longer, but she, like Jimmy, cannot help herself. Her grip on her role of mother is loosening as she toys with actually being his mother again. When Jimmy tries to kiss her in the Hall of Mirrors in the funhouse where they take refuge in a storm, Renee sees Sam standing at the door. When Jimmy asks her what's wrong, Renee responds by saying she has to go to rehearsal. Renee tries to remind herself that Jimmy's secret should remain so, if only because she is not willing to go back into rehearsals for the role of Sam's wife and Jimmy's mother.

Jimmy has decided he must make love to Renee to uncover the secret he still believes is hers. This corresponds to Rose's determination to "humanize" Jonner the elephant trainer by "giving herself to him," enduring his blundering attentions for the sake of his redemption. Will it hurt? Yes, but she hopes to gain Jonner's humanity through her sacrifice. Jimmy is uncertain whether he wants to go through the pain of becoming human, but steels himself to it. Again, it is the woman's act of giving which humanizes the man; it is painful but necessary to her task of endowing the male with a performance of manhood.

Jimmy invites Renee home, and she goes with him, looking around the old house as though within a dream. He tries to kiss her again, then tries to take off her blouse (reclaiming his once rightful, now forbidden, place at his mother's breast) and when she resists, he throws her out. Jimmy storms back to the kitchen and finds Renee's purse. He dumps it out onto the floor, and finds a picture of his parents, Renee in sunglasses, laughing. When Sam arrives, later, enough time has passed for Jimmy to have made up his story, which is that he actually knew all along that Renee was his mother, but couldn't help trying to possess her. When Sam tells Jimmy he just didn't have the nerve to tell him the truth about Renee, Jimmy responds by saying that if Sam had told him who Renee was everything would have been different.

Looking ahead to *The Crying Game*, there is an echo here of Fergus reproaching Dil for not telling him "who she was," and falling back on the idea that things would have been different if he had known--that he would not have fallen in love with her.[3] More importantly, Jimmy has taken refuge in the literary potential of his "story," translating his shock into the more appealing idea that, through dramatic foreshadowing, he knew all along, but was driven by fate to fulfill his Greek-tragic destiny. He has gotten into this habit in part from his association with Rose, whom, as he says earlier, will always give reasons for things, giving everything a history and a linear beginning-middle-end structure and the comfort such structure entails. But, more tellingly, his fiction is an attempt to perform an alternative reality, to enable himself to cope with his new understanding of his own identity. But he is unable to give himself this gift of performance, because he is unused to recognizing alternative selves as anything but fictions on paper. So he turns to Renee, making her tell the story of how she was performing onstage when she met Sam, how they endured a stormy relationship, how she left to save herself by creating a public identity. Renee knew Sam must have made up some story to explain her absence, but that she felt she had truly died when she found out Jimmy thought she was dead.

Or, when she realized her part had been definitively written out of Jimmy's life. Performance is life; for Renee, Jimmy represents a remainder of her past performance of wife and mother in Bray, and if he does not acknowledge that, by acknowledging her, then Renee loses some of her own life performance. This is why she seeks Jimmy out, especially after he first rejects her. It is not that Renee is dependent on the men she gives performance to, but that she must have her performance credited; for Sam to have erased her from Jimmy's life is to deny what she has given to both of them--a part of herself. This is what she feels Jimmy has a right to know--that although she did not perform traditional motherhood, she is still able to contribute to his development and sense of self. Again, in this way she is much like the disappeared yet powerful Rene of *The Past*. But

Renee Baker has to fight to have her performance, her enablement of her son, her audiences, and her fellow-performers, recognized and valued. Unlike Una, Renee unmakes her husband when she realizes he will never acknowledge her acting ability (acting again as Jordan's metaphor for performance). And unlike Rene O'Shaughnessy, Renee Baker will not let her performance be skewed toward a holy triangle of men in which she is reduced to passive spirit.

Jimmy falls asleep in a church after his interview with Renee, and when he wakes in the morning, he finds himself watched over by an elephant; circus animals run about freely as he walks to find Rose, who is standing still as animal tumult runs around her. She has stolen Jonner's keys while copulating and freed all the circus animals. Rose had claimed earlier that her aim was higher than Jimmy's, since he desired sex and she desired to free the animals. Rose can thus supply even animals with the opportunity to fulfill their essential natures, and Jimmy honors her achievement as they walk together. Rose relates her sex story as a scene from a novel, and the film closes on their good-natured argument about whether her hair was spread on the hay like a fan (Jimmy) or a seashell (Rose). Finally Jimmy must concede that it is Rose's hair, to describe as she will.

This concession is important, in that it reaffirms first that life is a constructed performance, and as susceptible to literary form and drama as any book because it is iterated in the same way by actual people that it is by books. Each person's partner(s) demand(s) an iteration of romantic or domestic behaviors that are supplied to the last detail by social norms. However, it also reaffirms that each person is in control of both the details of their performance and the interpretation of those details, as well as larger events. While the plot is affected by outside forces which cannot be averted or dictated to, each life can be made and re-made endlessly by those writing/living it. Jimmy's journey into adulthood goes from seeing fiction as completely removed from "real life," and trying to throw over that fictional existence for "real" experience (during which time he sees less of Rose), to incorporating the two concepts of "real" and "constructed," thus de-throning the drive for essence.

Jimmy's renewed closeness to Rose indicates that his continued involvement with "female" performance, uncertainty, constant re-writing and change will prevent him from continuing his effort to replicate or regain his lost relationship with his mother.

Jimmy is allowed to re-write his mother, not into his past, as someone dead to him, but into his present, as someone who supplied him with an understanding of performance and the real power of fictions. Unlike the narrator of *The Past*, Jimmy is able to accept the performance his mother gives him, and Renee is not lost in the mists of impersonal history, but permeates the possibilities of Jimmy's future. Sam, hopelessly moored in a past as fictional as any of Jimmy's and Rose's stories, refuses to allow Renee's performance to enable his own future, since he needs her to remain with him, constantly re-affirming his "essence" (music/musician) through her performance (singer). When Renee leaves the stage, Sam draws the curtain, even on Jimmy to a certain extent, and the divide between father and son is definite. This time, the lost mother reclaims her son.

> Ireland wanking is Ireland free.
> --*The Pornographer*

Michael O'Shaughnessy, James Vance, Old Mahoney, Moran and Sam Coleman are all given confidence and social importance by their roles as fathers. All five men strive to erase the original necessity of women to their current roles, reducing their wives to props, most of whom have long faded from memory. Rather than recognize their own function as props in others' lives (usually their own fathers') before their enablement, these men focus on re-writing their histories to show how they were always true to a self they always knew.

As if to illustrate the performative nature of male essence, in 1979, McGahern, hitherto praised for depicting the traditional rural Irish lifestyle so desperately enthroned in modern Ireland, published *The Pornographer*. There was immediate critical outcry against its vulgarity in Ireland, and immediate critical wonder at its currency in England and America.[4] Nominally the story of a young man who writes hack soft-core for a living who finally finds true love after a series of uncaring, shallow relationships by marrying a woman from the country and going to settle on his parents' farm, *The Pornographer* produces exactly the opposite story, a backlash against the enforced patriarchal nature of domesticity of Irish society.

The Pornographer's unnamed male protagonist defies women to shape his life or offer him a role in their own performance. An orphan, he has left his family, which consists of his aunt and uncle, to go to Dublin where he lives and works alone in his barren apartment. Though his parent's farmhouse still waits for him, kept righteously in the family by his aunt and uncle despite the many offers they receive for it, the protagonist refuses to visit the country. His aunt is terminally ill with cancer, and is hospitalized frequently in Dublin. His uncle goes down to see her, and so the protagonist is kept in closer contact with his relatives' guileless lifestyle than he would like; although he loves his aunt and uncle, he cannot but see them as snares set up by the domestic world. He feels guilty about his unwillingness to see his aunt, and is fearful of his uncle's tentative attempts to reclaim him for the farm. He has begun an affair with an unnamed older woman in which he is casual on commitment yet insistent on sexual relations, and sees this indeterminacy as a bid for freedom.[5] His older lover is a sheltered woman, a virgin when they meet, who tries to uphold the same liberated lifestyle as the protagonist but cannot. She lives in a boarding house and is anxious for a family of her own. She is also a travel writer, for a magazine called *Waterways*, and here McGahern points up the social textuality of their relationship by allowing both the protagonist and his lover to write stories from both ends of the social spectrum that intertwine and comment on each other.

  The protagonist writes a regular series about the sexual adventures of Mavis and Colonel Grimshaw for his publisher Maloney. We read the different episodes of this text several times, which follow a predictable pattern in different exotic locales. It is low-end pornography, replete with phrases like "iron-hard rod," "I want to see that gorgeous soft mound on high," and "Harder, hurt me, do anything you want with me, I'm crazy for it" (McGahern 1979, 23). When he is done, the writer comments: "I am tired and flushed as I get up from the typewriter. Nothing ever holds together unless it is mixed with some of one's own blood. I am not able to read what I've written. Will others be inflamed by the reading, if there is flesh to inflame, as I was by the poor writing? Is my flush the flesh of others, are my words to be their worlds?" (Ibid., 24).

  His lover's writing is not built for shock, yet she is just as invested in the world she creates for her readers, since they might really live in it if they go on the boat trips she writes about. She takes the protagonist on one of her trips, an evaluation of a pleasure cruise on the Shannon, and he tells her, "I was thinking how well you work.

That you make notes, write everything down. It's not that usual. You'd be surprised how many try to get by on that old amateurish flair" (89). It is one of the very few moments in which both parties are equal to each other, brought together in mutual craftsworkship. Shortly after the trip, she discovers she is pregnant and wants to be married; just after this, the protagonist, reeling with shock and denial toward the product of his sexual "freedom," writes up a pornographic account of their trip on the Shannon with Mavis and the Colonel taking their roles. The protagonist uses whole sets of dialogue from both the actual trip and his lover's story, interspersing it with sex and then, importantly, commenting on it with sex:

> 'Have you ever gone in for the girls, Michael?' the Colonel slapped [the boat's keeper] on the knee.
> 'Not in any serious way...it's all right for the rich. But my generation, seeing the hardship our parents had to go through, decided to stay clear. Maybe we were as well off. Anyhow we hadn't the worry.'
> 'No wonder the country is in such a poor state...An old boy like that, drinking all round the country, laughing at women, boasting he'd escaped--escaped from what?' (158, 159-160)

Suddenly the licentious Colonel sounds like an Irish moralist, and the crude boatsman voices the opinions of the liberal left. The Colonel trusses Michael up and Mavis rapes him; they leave him sleeping it off and Mavis says, "He'll think he was dreaming. Doesn't the whole country look as if it's wetdreaming its life away. He'll want to be no exception. He's a prime example of your true, conforming citizen" (161). This mighty didactic pornography is the voice of the female lover whispering doubts into the protagonist's mind; he realizes the emptiness of his random promiscuity. Yet he also realizes the equal emptiness of obeying form and convention without emotional commitment. His "sleazy" writing ends up as a comment on her wholesome, natural picture of life on the Shannon, seemingly so easy to obtain yet based in the purity and unreality of another, fictional world.

The female lover's role is a complex one: while, despite her brave foray into unmarried sex, she does not seek an enabling resistance to the status quo; her insistence on marriage and home-making are the spurs to the male protagonist's first realizations that he is as mired in emotion-deadening inaction as his lover is trapped in emotion-deadening conformity. He is "plagued by images" of the pre-planned domestic life waiting for him: "There was a semi-detached house...raspberry canes that needed cutting back...the narrow kitchen...the back garden, the formica-topped breakfast table, the radio, the clock, the whirring fridge...proudly, stretching towards the line and beaming benediction on the whole setup, she'd hang out her brand-washed flags as good as any" (103). The female lover's offer of traditional life is negative, but then again it's not so negative as the male lover's offer of the even more traditional ultimatum that she abort the baby or get out of his life. The female lover's insistence on marriage is primarily an insistence on involving the male lover in the consequences of their mutual action; she forces him to acknowledge his own double-standard. She cannot break out of the cycle of safe conformity which, to her in her understandably panicked state as a low-income, middle-aged, unwed, suddenly-pregnant Irish woman, offers her her only chance to make good her losses. This will be up to the nurse, the male protagonist's second lover, whom I shall return to later. For now, the importance of the first female lover is her shattering of the male lover's complacence. She offers no enabling resistive performance, but she prepares him for the lifesaving resistance which the nurse will later offer him.

Maloney, the protagonist's boss at the pornographic press, tells him repeatedly that he cannot get away with not marrying the woman, as this would be an escape from just punishment of his sins. The sins in questions are unlawful intercourse, possible abortion, and deserting the in-utero family he has helped to create. To Maloney, mimicking society's spokesmen, the protagonist's knowledge of his lover's pregnancy is equal to assuming responsibility for having a family: "You've sullied the Shannon and you're still out there laughing, back at square one, ready to start all over again. You need a lecture, all right. You need several lectures" (163). Later, when the pregnant lover leaves for London, Maloney tells the protagonist, "'You're our true Renaissance man, a true sophist. Inflaming people and fathering children which you later disown. Let me tell you this...we're not letting you off the hook. You've lowered the moral average all around. And you're making us all feel good'" (249-250). Maloney's good-natured yet real resentment of the protagonist's "escape" from marriage springs in part from the fact that Maloney himself was married because he got his lover pregnant.

Although he is tempted to take the safe route by such social pressures, as well as by his lover's tenderness toward him, the male protagonist cannot finally commit to marriage simply because of the social security it offers. Though he would like to have love and even a family, he cannot just walk into a performance tailor-made and impatiently held out by the state. The protagonist's final refusal to share the performance of home and hearth his lover desires causes her to at last go to London, where she will have the baby without him at the home of an expatriate Irish family, the Kavanaghs.

Even as the expecting lover's letters implore him to visit her and claim his child, and report the ire of the Kavanaghs toward his unnatural behavior, the protagonist meets another woman, an unnamed nurse from the hospital where his aunt is being treated for her incurable cancer. On their first date, the nurse asks him if he would like to be married, and to his startled return of the question answers, "Of course I would. To have my own husband and child and house and garden and saucepans and pets. All that." She adds that she would not marry "a boring man" (174). The protagonist is wary, hearing her name exactly the material incentives for marriage that he despises. But he finds that she is different; she is not a virgin, she uses birth control, and she will not confuse sex with love.

The nurse's responsible, consciously political resistance to the very powerful coercion of the Irish state to remain chaste and to marry and stop working contributes to the protagonist's growing realization that his promiscuity was really not much of a resistance at all. In fact, he was playing into the hands of the status quo first by keeping sex outside marriage risky for women (he did not use contraception), and then by blaming and ostracizing the woman because of her pregnancy. The sexual responsibility shown by the nurse reflects badly on the protagonist's essentializing of sex as a universal, apolitical need which must be gratified. In fact, the protagonist is forced to realize that, scandalous occupation aside, he has actually been approximating the essential Irish farmer in his sexual rutting and his objectification of women.

After a few dates with the nurse, the protagonist sees his former lover in London, who still offers him marriage. He comes back frightened off women and the commitment they represent, and avoids the nurse, who confronts him with his irresponsibility--not in the usual way, emphasizing his social duty to marry her, but on the level of emotional integrity. He made a promise to be honest to her and she demands he keep it, not because it is his role in society to prop her up, but because he is an adult who ought to keep the promises he makes. In fact, the nurse engages the protagonist in his first adult relationship, helping him make the crucial break from the cyclical fate of marrying because he can do nothing else (evidenced by Michael and James in *The Past*). He agrees to fulfill his promise and his integrity and tells her about the woman in London who is having his baby. Her objective reaction to his situation forces him to see it through to the end, and also signals the beginning of his ability to feel real emotions other than fear and guilt--namely, tenderness and a longing for the nurse which is not purely sexual. Her refusal to allow the protagonist to slip into his old role of casual lover, he-who-feels-nothing, enables her to protect the independence of her own identity-performance in the relationship and challenges him to reconsider the validity of his own.

In a sense, he is dependent upon the affection of the women he is with to give him something to reject--he sees their "unwanted" love as a concrete example of the social forces pushing them together. Now he cannot reject the "other." If the new relationship fails, he will have only himself to blame. In this spirit, he goes to London one last time when the baby is born, refuses to marry his ex-lover and is beaten up by Mr. Kavanagh. On his return to Ireland, he finds that his aunt has died. The first event closes his feelings of responsibility toward his ex-lover, the second allows him to feel grief where grief is called for.

This emotionalism spurs him to new awareness of the beauty of domestic materials when they function as tools in a happy relationship. When he goes into his uncle's home before his aunt's funeral, he sees domesticity in quite a new light:

> It was a big slated nineteenth-century farmhouse, five front windows and a solid hall door looking confidently down on the road...It was very warm in the kitchen, and the first thing he did was to shake down the Stanley and pile in more coal. Blue and whit mugs hung from hooks on the deal dresser, and an oilcloth in blue and white squares covered the big deal table. Wedding and baptismal photos, even one ordination group, hung with the religious pictures around the tall walls. I found it very lovely. (233)

His uncle offers him the farmhouse again, and now the protagonist decides to take it. When he tells Maloney he is going to quit his job, marry his new lover, and move into his family's house in the country, he states that "There comes a time when you either run amok completely or try to make a go of it...I'm going to try to make a go of it" (250-251). Ironically, he has realized that his former Don Juanism was as programmatic as marriage itself, with its ages-old rules and demands. Ireland wanking is not necessarily Ireland free. He has decided to pursue a real relationship with the nurse, whom he plans to marry. The nurse's refusal to provide a purely sexual identity for the protagonist forces him first to admit to his lack of purpose, almost a lack of personhood, and then to create his own role in the world of adult relationships. He will be a father and a husband, but these roles will be self-fashioned, and not completely dependent upon a woman's ability to keep fueling his own sense of who he is.

He first realizes this when he is visiting his aunt for the last time: "And the dark-haired girl [the nurse], and the woman with child in London, the dying woman I was standing beside...what of them? The answer was in the vulgarity of the question. What of yourself?" (203). The protagonist discovers what none of McGahern's male characters before him has understood, that to be satisfying, one's identity must offer something to the performances around it which help to define it--his performance of husband and father and lover must give as much to the female's domestic performances as it takes from it. This reciprocal relationship allows for the shaking off of adolescent preoccupations with parents and the domesticity they represent, as well as an eliding of the stagnance of state-prescribed domesticity.

"There is pure reaction without reflection": Critical Takes

Karlheinz Schwartz's comment from his article "John McGahern's Point of View" is not made on critical reactions to McGahern's texts--it describes the pornographer's lifestyle--but it serves to define their general nature (Schwartz 1984, 108). I will focus perforce on reaction to McGahern's novels, as contemporary critical reception of *The Miracle* was overwhelmingly limited to plot-retellings and movie blurbs, and later critics of Jordan's works have been equally disinclined to make substantial comment on the text of the movie. Therefore, I am limited to examining critical responses to McGahern.

Those who admired *The Pornographer* did so on the basis of either deprecating Irish ignorance and prudery or applauding happy escapes from domesticity, while those who disliked the book based their dislike on the negativity of McGahern's "vision."[6] Shaun O'Connell's article "Door Into the Light: John McGahern's Ireland" and Michael J. Toolan's "John McGahern: The Historian and the Pornographer" are two examples of negative reaction; despite the fact that O'Connell likes the novels.

As O'Connell reads *The Pornographer*, he makes constant reference to "the moist valleys of Roscommon," intimately and immediately associating Ireland with the first female lover, both as fundamentally pornographic women who problematize male action: "Josephine [see note] comes to represent something deeply, darkly Irish to her 30 year-old lover...John Updike was right to note 'the hero's deadly coldness, and Josephine's credible, vital humanity,' but he misses some of her threat...she comes to stand for Irish conformity" (O'Connell 1984, 265).

Irish conformity, of course, being the prudishly domestic--in accordance with the "national character." The protagonist's conformity to the promiscuity which demands "the refusal of emotional commitment [leading] to entropy" is not a factor in O'Connell's reading, which relies upon a dichotomy between good women and bad (Prescott 1979, 108). Josephine, the first lover, is a bad woman because she threatens her man with a conformity rooted deep in her Irish "nature." The nurse, however, is a good woman, for "the glory that the pornographer holds in the nurse's body is the promise of renewal through love and sex" (O'Connell 1984, 267).

Again, female enablement is female virtue, and while O'Connell notes this enablement he does not unpack its consequences, namely the possibility of new male and female performances of domesticity made possible by male adaptation of female resistance performances. Instead, women are only positive forces when subjugating themselves to traditional men and goals, and O'Connell continues to locate regressive tendencies of chaos and failure in feminized, pornographic, modern Ireland: "Failed reporter, failed lover, cynic, dandy, aesthete, Maloney's mutability embodies modern Ireland's openness" (Ibid., 266). Thus O'Connell reduces the plot to that of canny man resisting evil woman until right woman comes along, and his reading amounts to a negation at best and an overlooking at worst of what power it is that "right" woman possesses which can rescue a man from himself.

Toolan's negative reading of *The Pornographer* is based on his rejection of what he sees as McGahern's failure to live up to his commitment to "the healing and transcendent power of love," apparently promised by the "happy" ending of McGahern's earlier novel *The Leavetaking*, the story of marriage based on reciprocal need for parent-figure spouses (Toolan 1981, 30). Toolan sums up those arguments when he asks why, "in opposition to the bright, vital ...optimism of *The Leavetaking*...of the possibility of liberation from an imprisoning past, McGahern will compulsively return to a dark, bleak world of narrow expectations and stunted hopes...in which frustrated impulses are not only accepted, *but actually structure and shape the lives of the protagonists*" (my italics--Ibid., 40). Toolan resists exactly the definition of performance, the idea that formal iteration of social norms dictates what actions and resistances can/will be made by those whose pasts, presents, and futures are iterated within/by those norms. Insisting instead on the humanist tradition of self-determination by unified individuals, Toolan cannot understand why McGahern "undertakes a willful perversion of his fictional [sic] gifts...to damningly evoke the sterility and perversion, the deadliness and bestiality, of the lives of the characters in the fiction" (40-41). In assigning sterility, perversion, deadliness and bestiality only to "characters in the fiction," Toolan rejects the same application of fiction to actual life. Thus the idea that human lives are as much the products of state tinkering as fictional lives are the products of authorial tinkering is "inhuman"--and the shaping influence of modern nationalism, underlined by performative resistance, is elided.

It is important that marriage is still validated by McGahern's texts--in *The Pornographer* as well as in *Amongst Women* and the other texts that will be discussed below. Because the institution is strongly associated with negative traditions of oppressed women and unselfconscious men does not necessarily mean that it must be abandoned, but that it must be revolutionized. While Jordan will move away from traditional marital relations in the works studied below, McGahern will keep his characters working within it. However, Jordan will continue to focus on parent-child relationships, even outside of a traditional story line, as we shall see in the discussion of *The Dream of A Beast* below. This reflects the individual differences between the authors as well as a political difference; for while Jordan finds himself hampered by traditional structures, both literally (the novel) and figuratively (heterosexual courtship and marriage narratives), because they are shaped by traditional representations of gender roles, McGahern finds the traditional channels of representation offering a more and more compelling way into the subtext of surface normality. In Jordan, male characters seeking relief from abnormality in their lives by turning to relationships with women are duly surprised when those relationships overturn all the usual definitions of normal. In McGahern, this realization is not always so strong, but it is there, not only for the men who seek traditional relationships but for the women who think they can provide them.

Notes

    1. The screenplay of *The Miracle* is currently unavailable in the US; I would have quoted from the movie directly but as Miramax, which holds copyright on *The Miracle*, has strict policies banning the use of the text without authorial consent, I have had to rely on paraphrase of the dialogue.

    2. Jordan seems to use these two names to represent stereotypes of Irish and non-Irish. The name "Rene(e)" is repeated from *The Past*, where is it described as not Irish-sounding (50-51); so also the exotic American Renee shares the name. "Jimmy" is the typically "Irish" name, used by Fergus when he wants to blend in as a "Pat," and by Jimmy Coleman when he is not trying to impress Renee with his maturity (when he uses "James").

    3. Neil Jordan. 1993. *The Crying Game*. In *The Neil Jordan Reader*. New York: Routledge, 237-238.

    4. See John Naughton (1979), Peter Prescott (1979), and Karlheinz Schwartz (1984) for reactions which focus on the currentness of the plot. See Tom Paulin (1980), Shaun O'Connell (1984), and Toolan (1981) for negative reactions to the subject matter.

    5. In the earliest edition of *The Pornographer*, the lover is given the name Josephine. I am using the more definitive later edition, in which the namelessness of all the main characters is uniform and pertinent. Later critics cited in this chapter sometimes refer to the lover by this name.

    6. Naughton (1979), Prescott (1979), O'Neill (1979) and Mano (1980) all give the book positive reviews, and, with the exception of O'Neill, matter-of-factly revile what they are content to see as "typical" Irish backwardness as they do so.

Chapter Four

The Private Performer--Domestic Women's Resistance

> She did not try to defend herself...
> Not once did she protest at the unfairness.
> She seemed willing to go to almost any length
> to appease, lull his irritation to rest, contain all
> the exasperation by taking it within herself.
> This usually redoubled it.
> --*Amongst Women*

For all his swagger and centrality, Moran is not the main character of *Amongst Women*. His second wife, Rose, is a supportive yet unsettling presence in the Moran household, and provides a fascinating and complex representation of the kinds of resistance to marginalization the domestic Irish woman is capable of performing. If I elided Rose from my analysis of the dynamics of the father-figure in *Amongst Women*, it is because Rose merits separate consideration as the woman who at once suffers, supports and undermines the often brutal husband she has chosen. In this respect she is much like Dil in Jordan's film *The Crying Game*; a woman seemingly trained to lower her expectations when it comes to men but who actually uses traditional relationships to enable her own embattled female identity.

For both Rose and Dil, being a woman means being at the service of a man. Yet both choose to deliberately put themselves into relations with men, despite the personal cost. Perhaps this is because both characters realize that supporting a man means that man's authority is undermined through his very reliance on his woman. And for these women--lower-class, alone, without the glamour of stage-fame or the mystique of superior spirituality—something more than co-dependence leads to their ultimate dominance of that minor yet crucial stage, the family, and the personal relationships which maintain it.

Standing By: The Woman behind the Man

> ...there was blanket condemnation of us putting through this bill, which was in essence to try in some way to acknowledge the non-financial contribution of the [female] spouse to the matrimonial home and to give [her] a type of ownership, to put it in most simple terms (Burton, et al. 1994, 15).
> --Helen Keough on the 1994 Irish Family Law Property Bill

Rose Brady's advent into the life of the Moran household is presented as a crucial disjuncture in Moran's program of unchallenged domestic rule. From the start, we know little about Rose, save that she is in her late thirties, unmarried, and returned to Ireland from a domestic job in Scotland. Given her age and marital status, Rose is assumed by her family and village to be a confirmed, albeit dignified, spinster. But when she escapes the quiet of her mother's home one night and meets Moran at the post office, Rose determines almost immediately to pursue him and carefully manifests behaviors that, according to social more, commit herself and Moran to eventual marriage. Mrs. Brady is immediately wary of her daughter's slightest involvement with Moran, and her opinion of Rose's chances for happiness with such a man echo those held by the village, and perhaps the reader, in general:

> 'They say he's no ornament,' her mother said carefully.
> 'I was talking to him in the post office.'
> She saw her mother look at her sharply. 'They say he's one sort of person when he's out in the open among people--he can be very sweet--but that he's a different sort of person altogether behind the walls of his own house.'
> 'People talk too much about other people round here. Often the talk is just ignorant malice.' (McGahern 1990, 24)

Indeed, Rose seems determined to turn a blind eye to common knowledge about Moran, and this determination to bind her fate to that of the village monster sets her up for tragedy in the public's eye. Because Moran has so completely established his reputation as a miserly, spiteful hermit, to those in the world outside Great Meadow Rose can only be understood as a spinster driven into a living hell of abuse by her need to marry. It is assumed she will fare as poorly as the pitiable Moran children, under the thrall of their tyrannical father and subject to his every whim.

But from her first entrance into the story--into Moran's story--Rose is anything but a victim, and she chooses her husband carefully and deliberately, objectively weighing Moran's merits according to her own standards, which are far remote from those of a desperate, romantic spinster. From her first encounter with Moran at the post office, Rose assesses him in conjunction with his material possessions, seeing each as a new revelation of his separateness from the community and its common run of men. She has walked past and noted his stone house and large fields, and when he drives to her mother's house to pay a visit,

> 'I didn't know you had a car,' she said with surprise when they reached the road.
> ...Secretly she exulted that he had the car. It was just one more sign of his separateness from the people around who would buy a cow or a few more fields. In these parts a car was prized more than flowers or an orchard or a [sic] herb garden: it was the symbol of pure luxury. (30)

This is not to imply that Rose is after Moran for his money, at least not in the usual sense. What she wants, however, might seem far more sinister to Moran--Rose wants to share in his power.

For Rose immediately understands that Moran, rather than a hermit or a madman, is a powerful man, powerful enough, in the first place, to separate himself from society and live as he chooses while still commanding an awed respect from that abandoned, scorned society. He has brought up his family by himself, kept them financially secure seemingly through sheer will power alone, and, because he has asked for no one's help in this, he is in no one's debt. His personal power is uncontested. Therefore in the uniformly drab, small world of the rural Irish farming village, Moran stands out as an exciting, dynamic force to which Rose is immediately attracted. The car is a symbol of his ability to think beyond the world of the small-hold farmer, just as his unfailingly careful dress, whether at home or away, is a symbol of Moran's consciousness of himself as more than just a farmer--he is a pillar of the nation, and although he is extremely private, he is a public figure. The éclat his bravery earned him thirty years ago during the Civil War is maintained now by his aloof, commanding presence.

Given Rose's background and experiences, Moran is the only acceptable choice of husband for her. She has been living in Glasgow as at once the governess of the Rosenbloom children and the sophisticated companion of Mrs. Rosenbloom, mixing easily in the best company. Working behind "the usual social frameworks: family, position, conventions, those established forms," Rose "could work with a charm and singleness of attention that became so smooth as to be chilling, except for the friendliness of her large grey eyes. The Rosenblooms had long known that they could take her with them anywhere in society" (24). Yet Rose longs to return to Ireland and have a home and a family of her own. The basis of this desire goes well beyond feminine instinct, however; in her desire for her own place, Rose is asserting a desire for a share of the domestic power upon which Ireland is now predicated. Her situation in the Rosenbloom family is a parallel structure: she attains domestic prestige in a foreign household but it does not empower her, as it is conferred upon her by dint of hired service; what Rose desires is a domestic power which cannot be rescinded because it springs from the unshakable position of wife and mother. In her own home, she must always belong, and she will be able to exert her own will, impossible when one is a servant, no matter how beloved. Rose desires access to the law which is the household in Ireland; more importantly, she desires to wield that law rather than just receive it. Although the father is the family head who is granted power in Irish society, Rose wants to extend that power to the mother by becoming the female voice which can speak for the family by virtue of her unchallenged partnership with the father.

Rose captures the fairly willing Moran. For Moran, "Rose Brady's attention had been as unexpected as it had been sudden and welcome. It was as if she had fallen out of a generous sky...his life could glow again in the concentration of her attention" (26-27). What Moran expects of his new wife is someone who will enable him to maintain his single control over his family. But what he is about to get from Rose is someone who wants to participate in maintaining control over a shared family; someone who wants to be an equal partner in keeping the Moran household running, separate and important. Rose does not intend to blend into Moran's shadow as his children have. Rather, she intends to take on the mantle of his power, to be recognized as Rose Moran of Great Meadow, to have the respect afforded Moran conferred on her as well. Rose loves Moran for his own sake, but what she most loves and respects is his position as an

Irish man--landowning, self-sufficient, head of a family. In this way, Rose is a staunch supporter of the patriarchal nature of the Republic she returns to. She has no wish to subvert the social hierarchy. What she may or may not realize is that by taking part in patriarchy as a woman, Rose cannot help subverting it. She is prepared to put up with abuse from Moran not because she wishes to efface herself, but because she consents to the social order which demands that a wife be at her husband's beck and call. But in return for her service, she assumes that she will be given her own share of the father's power, and in the end, this is what she achieves.

This pattern of what can be called conformative resistance is not restricted to the literary household in Ireland. Flesh-and-blood Irish women perform this sort of resistance through appropriation on a widespread and regular basis, as is evidenced by the structure and tactics of women's social and political groups in Ireland (and the prevailing tendency of the social to develop into the political).[1] Anne Mulvey is one of many observers who document the grassroots, proudly domestic character of women's organizations in Ireland, members of which gladly enter into marriage and motherhood because they have come to feel the household is their birthright; shared with their husbands, but on an equal-partner basis within which ownership devolves upon wives as well as husbands. The household necessarily remains tied to marriage, but Mulvey claims this does not hinder Irish women's ability to reform these institutions even as they value them: literally, as landowners; and figuratively, as Mothers and the traditional Woman. Such "traditional" women create organizations which "reflect feminist values better than other (U.S.) Women's Studies [groups]...in that [they] seemed more inclusive of women who were not academics, and...reached a more diverse cross-section of Irish women--including working-class and poor women" (Mulvey 1992, 508). Household ownership is one of the few--perhaps the only--powerfully enabling status which cuts across all class lines in Ireland; because it is recognized as a commonly-held value, all women can potentially attempt to access it, and therefore organize themselves into groups which preserve this value but work to make it more equitable.

As Rose grows more and more powerful within the Moran household, Moran withers, for despite Rose's firm backing of Moran as head of the household, his reliance on a woman's affirmation of his power diminishes it. In a society which depends upon silenced women to perpetuate male power, a man who lets a woman speak for him is silenced. From the start of their relationship Rose imperceptibly alters Moran's behaviors in order to make a place for herself in his world. To court her Moran must visit her home, and take her to a public outing; in short, he must enter her world of social convention, and rely upon her judgment. "Was I alright in the house?" he asks her after his visit to her home, and she replies, "You were perfect" (McGahern 1990, 29). At a Christmas dance before their marriage, Rose makes her position clear:

> Rose had come to the dance to claim their place as a couple among the people in this loose, Christmas carnival. She was determined to remain. She smiled and chatted with everybody around her. She took tea. ...She forced Moran to dance and by the night's end she was worn out by the single effort. He had given her no help throughout the night but it did not lessen her love. (37)

The last point is important. By making a public show of her relation to Moran, Rose is not trying to force Moran into the public world, to lessen his isolation. Exactly the opposite: Rose is showing the public world that she is now part of the special, separate world of Great Meadow, that she has a claim on Moran and has therefore gained in stature by virtue of her association with him. She must be treated as Moran is treated, with unusual respect. Rose will not try to enforce this respect with threatened violence, as Moran does; she uses her tact and friendliness to make others, including Moran's children, accept her new position of authority. But her will to that power is as iron as Moran's, and it is this similar drive that she expects will please her new husband.

The effect of Rose's arrival at the Moran house is best immediately ascertained by the children, who realize that "the life they had come to know so well for so long as it slipped by changelessly would be irrevocably altered: it was like a death or a wounding and brought all the wonder and fear and awe of change" (38). Again, although Rose has no desire to change life at Great Meadow but only to become part of it and help it to continue, her very advent into the patriarchy of the household irremediably alters it. The children's very affection for Rose is a mitigation of the singleness of their affection for their father. An argument in the first months of marriage makes clear Rose's progression from expendable wife/servant to unquestioned, irreplaceable, powerful member of the family.

This argument takes place after an incident with the children. Their help in the fields, undertaken while Rose is out visiting her mother, fires in Moran a resentment against Rose as outsider. "We could get on topping without her," he says to the children. Soon after, as Rose is cleaning, Moran says "quietly as if he were taking rifle aim, 'There's no need for you to go turning the whole place upside down. We managed well enough before you ever came around the place'" (68-69). Rose's response is to withdraw from Moran, and when, unnerved by her independence, Moran approaches her alone, she says,

>'I'll have to go away from here.'
>'I never heard such nonsense,' he blustered. ...
>'I was told I was no use in the house. I couldn't go on living in a place where I was no use,' she spoke with the quietness and desperate authority of someone who had discovered they could give up no more ground and live.
>'God, O God...I never meant anything like that. The whole world knows that the house was never run right until you came. A blind man could see that the children think the earth of you.'
>...'I love you dearly and I love the house but I couldn't live here if am not wanted.' (71)

Indeed it would be impossible for Rose to stay if she is not to be granted the authority her work in the household confers upon her. She must be recognized as a partner, as someone necessary to the Moran household, second only to Moran in importance and definitely removed from the level of the children into the higher realm of Parent. The ground she cannot give up is not her personal self-esteem so much as her place within the upper-echelon of the family. When Moran is forced to admit that his household was not run properly under his single care, he is admitting a very great deal; in fact, he is granting Rose the authority she demands. By doing so, he is relinquishing the power his completely solitary control of the family and house which attracted Rose to him.

This passage is crucial, for when Rose forces Moran to apologize, she is forcing him to acknowledge that she must be taken into account. Unlike the children, she cannot be bullied. But although Rose demands his respect, and a share in his power, she does not demand Moran's place in the family--that of the unquestioned head. This may seem a contradictory point, but it is not, for if she is to share in Moran's prestige and power, she must openly, publicly evince respect for that power. She cannot undermine Moran and then expect to partake in the respect he commands. Moran must be acknowledged by Rose as unshakably in charge so that all he stands for can be in turn associated to Rose herself. In short, Rose cannot debase what she plans to inherit.

This reading diverges from standard critical evaluations of the novel, which depict a cowed Rose as reduced by her husband to the same level as his children. Antoinette Quinn, who in her perceptive essay "A Prayer for My Daughters: Patriarchy in *Amongst Women*," intelligently assesses the power of Rose's submission to Moran, still reads Rose as almost immediately trapped by her own clever plan to subvert Moran's authority:

> ...Rose's ploy of allying herself with Moran's daughters is interpreted more negatively: 'Then, like a shoal of fish moving within a net, Rose and the girls started to clear the table...' (*Amongst Women* 79). The image catches the empathy between Rose and her step-daughters but also portrays all the women as victims, trapped in the tense atmosphere which Moran generates. A shift in power relations has occurred and Rose is no longer in control. Her status is equal with that of Moran's children. (Quinn 1991, 81)

Quinn states that Rose is fighting Moran for power, for her place in the house, and concludes that Rose ends up "settling for...the limited right to be treated like a member of the Moran's family, to swim like a fish in his net" (Quinn 1991, 79). I believe the battle metaphor, though encouraged by the text in places, is crucially inaccurate, for it implies that Rose is in direct opposition to Moran, struggling to defeat him and his household, rather than trying to share his power within that household, and the larger world as well.

But Rose, perhaps, does not see this hourglass effect of power slipping from Moran to herself. She considers Moran and herself as equal sharers in a household power they both respect, in contrast to the changing values of the next generation--if not exactly equal, they are allies. But patriarchal power cannot be infiltrated or taken over by a woman and remain unchanged, and Rose succeeds in doing what she forbids the children and the world at large to do; she undermines Moran's self-confidence. If Rose can run the farm on her own, what good is he? What is his purpose? As Rose grows in her sense of being a partner in the patriarchal Ireland of Moran, she demands that that patriarchy be respected; she has paid her dues to the system and wants to receive her benefits. But as they age, Rose and Moran encounter more and more the younger generation's dismissal of the old ways. When, near the close of the novel, Rose and Moran are ignored by a bank manager, it is Rose who is upset:

> Several times Rose looked anxiously at Moran. If this had happened when they had first met he would have been up and out of [the] office long ago. Instead he continued sitting dejectedly and a little tiredly, not looking around him...Once out on the pavement it was Rose who was beside herself with anger.
> 'I never saw such manners in my life.'
> 'Who cares anyhow?' Moran said. 'Nobody cares.'
> 'I care,' she said passionately.
> 'That doesn't count. Nobody bothers these days.' (McGahern 1990, 175)

Rose's anger is for Moran's dignity, and for her own, as a sharer in his class. Moran's listlessness is not just the result of tired old age, but also of his diminishment in comparison to Rose. He senses that part of his inability to demand that his importance be acknowledged is rooted in his feeling that that importance has been transferred not only to the next generation, the young, but to Rose. He has little desire to assert himself because he now, at last, lets Rose represent him. She will confront the bank manager, she will rage to daughters Mona and Sheila. Rose has become interchangeable with Moran, they both equally represent him and his interests. Soon after this incident, Moran dies.

Unlike Una O'Shaughnessy, Rose Moran does not intend to mold her husband, to shape his destiny, to dictate and control how he will be remembered. She does not mock the male politics of her nation. Rose Moran wants most to uphold those politics which honor the heads of the household, and honor the household itself as the most important social unit. What she does want is to have the Mother recognized as as much a parent, an upholder of the household, as the Father. Rose's many defenses of Moran's tyrannical behavior are made on the basis that he is doing what's best for the family, the household; as a woman Rose needs that household structure because it is the only avenue of empowerment available to her. As a wife and mother she has a place in Irish society. She is therefore willing to support the system that gives her that place, despite the fact of the dubious role it allots to women, because she intends to redeem that dubious role to the extent of her powers.

Does Rose's very desire to wield the political and social power granted the head of the household ultimately undermine that power and the system behind it? When Moran allows his wife's voice to speak for him, he silences himself proportionately; thus Rose destroys the person she most admires. Yet she preserves the status she stands to inherit. In this way, female performance within (or, in a sense, of) patriarchy can invalidate not quite patriarchy itself, but rather its traditional agents--men. Female representation of the patriarchal Irish household is the most complete denial of male fitness to perpetuate that household. But it is not a denial of the importance or desirability of the household and, by extension, the domestic. The possibility that Rose Moran merely steps into a position of power within a system which remains oppressive to other less fortunate or strong-willed women remains open in the text. The conflicting dynamics of domestic power are coming to be the focus of many texts by women writing in and about patriarchal and/or post-colonial societies.

Contemporary women's world literature comments on the growing number of women who, accustomed to being at once a central metaphor in the rhetoric of freedom and excluded by actual political change, find themselves gaining a kind of power within the household which is unacknowledged by the state. Anyi Wang's *Lapse of Time* (China, 1984), Fay Weldon's *The Heart of the Country* (England, 1987), Sara Suleri's *Meatless Days* (Pakistan, 1987), and Hanan al-Shaykh's *Women of Sand and Myrrh* (Saudi Arabia, 1989) are just a few recent novels which chronicle the growing uncertainty of women who function as the heads in all but name of patriarchal households and whose pride in and empowerment through this covert ownership is threatened at once by official (male) sanctions against powerful women and the reproaches of those women who are not able to make the attempt to change the system from within.

At the close of *Amongst Women*, the ambiguity of the text concerning whether Rose realizes the destructive power of her support of the patriarch reaches its final impact. As the daughters and widow are leaving the gravesite after Moran's funeral, McGahern leaves the reader with a picture of female empowerment:

The men followed the bereaved women out of the graveyard at a hesitant, respectful distance, unsure of their place in the mourning.
But as the small tight group of stricken women slowly left...they seemed with every step to be gaining in strength...their first love and allegiance had been pledged...to this one house and man...Now not only had

they never broken that pledge but they were renewing it for a second time with this other woman who had come in among them and married him...now...it was as if each of them in their different ways had become Daddy...
'Poor Daddy,' Rose echoed absently out of her own thoughts before waking and turning brightly toward the girls. ...
'Will you look at the men. They're more like a crowd of women,' Sheila said...'The way Michael...is getting Sean and Mark to laugh you'd think they were coming from a dance.' (183-184)

I quote at length from the last pages of the book to show the closing message, which seems clearly to be that Rose has successfully taken on Moran's mantle of power and in so doing, allows his daughters to partake in that partially-feminized authority themselves, as they pledge their loyalty to Rose by virtue of her status as representative of the family and now, after his death, of Moran himself. This identification with Rose further allows the daughters to "become Daddy," thus finally diffusing Moran's identity into a group of four women. These empowered women then react to the men, whom they judge as Moran would have done, on the basis of their lack of respect and improper behavior; the men become "more like women" as the women become more like the man whose authority they have come to embody and feminize. One feels that Rose will continue to rule over Great Meadow, her presence calling the children back for visits, unharmed by the passing of Moran.

In contrast, Quinn's reading of the conclusion is more negative, as she views the Moran women as unwitting inheritors of evil:

> In view of the novel's critique of patriarchy, the desirability of the daughters' patrimony, however lyrically endorsed, is questionable, and it is finally questioned. The power they derive from their father is founded on dominance, not on the metaphysical revelations of his last months. It is an empowering that will enable them to live independently as adults, but it is also an assimilation of patriarchal values...we are given a glimpse of what becoming Daddy means. A reversal of gender roles takes place as brother and husbands, seen from a patriarchal perspective, are transformed into wives...Their [the daughters'] exclusiveness as Morans of Great Meadow is such that it does not even embrace their own husbands and children. (Quinn 1991, 89-90)

I do not aim to completely contradict the pessimistic reading Quinn demonstrates, for her analysis of McGahern's desire to de-romanticize Irish patriarchy/patriarchal families is quite valid; however, I believe that one crucial way McGahern's texts achieve this de-romanticization and questioning is by substituting women into traditional male roles and letting female influence alter the system, whether deliberately (the nurse in *The Pornographer*) or not (Rose Moran). Active, specifically modern women thus represent a changing Ireland. But the idea that a "reversal of gender roles" takes place not only elides evidence within the plot of the story but, more critically, it ignores the complexity of the problem the text presents. The text is at pains to point out that the Moran women follow a conscious program of embracing their husbands and children, especially Sheila, whose commitment to raising her children in a loving, positive, safe environment leads her to deliberately keep her children away from Moran (McGahern 1990, 169-170). In fact, the Moran women do not so much "become Daddy" as Moran becomes the women, since his legacy is carried on--in different ways--by them. Perhaps it is an inkling of this that causes Moran to begin to fear his daughters in his old age, as is stated at the outset of the novel.

Yet it remains a vexed question. The women do not take on the male role of distant, enigmatic, insular power figure. Nor, crucially, do the men surrender their social power to their wives. There is no way, I would state, that women can see men from the same "patriarchal perspective" as would another man; yet Rose's story points up at length that while patriarchs can be deposed by women, patriarchal ideals cannot be utterly undercut by women who support the patriarchal system. But I would argue that the very uncertainty of this political grey area is a fruitful departure from airtight readings of the text, whether they deny the power of female performance or insist on the binary-flipping power of that performance.

The most important, most revolutionary point is that Moran's legacy is not inherited intact, by either the men or the women; its power has been broken. The text works to show that the lines of inheritance are irrevocably tangled by the changed role of the domestic woman, whose advent into the ownership of the household alters the nature of patriarchal social structure yet raises questions about the possibility of completely undercutting patriarchy even as it situates it amongst women.[2]

What's the Funny Thing?:
The Man Behind the Woman Behind the Man

> Maybe you don't care whether you die or not.
> But consider the girl, Fergus. The wee black chick.
> --*The Crying Game*

In *The Crying Game*, another type of empowerment through heterosexual union is presented, in the relationship between Dil and Fergus. Taking place in England, this coupling of a lower-class black woman and a runaway Irish terrorist, respectively, has a special significance, for their union allows both of them to overcome their roles as racial others. While the question/questioning of Dil's sexuality has been the focus of most analyses of the film,[3] I want to focus more closely here on the racial and therefore class-oriented barriers to Dil's relationship with Fergus which are presented as actually more intractable than the barriers of "suspect" sexuality.

Because while the text[4] provides obvious instances of marked sexual ambiguity and comment, these are subordinate to the at-times more subtle yet absolutely pervasive racial tensions and comment which divide the characters. Race is much more clearly and importantly marked in the text than is sexuality, and I argue that this is because *The Crying Game* is a thoroughly post-colonial text, working its way through both colonial injustice and the desire to exact revenge on the colonizers once they are thrown off. The IRA (both as literary subtext and physical reality) is nothing if not a result of nation-building in Ireland, dedicated to separating Irish identity from British identity and keeping the British out of Ireland. So the racial tension in the film marks it as post-colonial; not only does white Irish racism come into play, when Jody remarks on the racism he encounters as a black man, but English racism against the Irish. Each sexual and possibly sexual encounter in the text is marked and dis/enabled by its racial and by extension its class context. This is the consequence of setting the action and characters within the context of the civil war in Northern Ireland--for even in England, Fergus is marked by his nationality. This choice of setting is, of course, not accidental. I posit that Jordan's text relies upon its deployment of familiar racial tensions in order to deflect some of the hostile attention given to its less socially-acceptable sexual tensions. And while those celebrated sexual tensions in the film are somewhat resolved--first by

Fergus' attraction to Jody and then by Fergus' successful relationship with Dil--the racial hatreds are never even bridged. I shall show below how Dil's sexual otherness defrays her racial otherness in Fergus' eyes; without the mitigating factor or her sexual difference Dil runs the risk of remaining too much a part of the hated English culture to be loved.

When I refer to "racism" in this analysis, I am referring not only to racism between black and white characters, but also to the hatred between the Irish and English which, over the course of centuries, has become an obvious, undeniable, self-proclaimed racial hatred. The hostilities between the two white nationalities have long been described as racist, going back at least to the monkey-caricatures of the Irish in Punch and other English magazines in the nineteenth century, and in English political tracts going well back into the sixteenth century, in which the Irish regularly perform the function of a different race, biologically opposed to the English. The habit of looking upon their near neighbors as racially inferior is thus a long-established English tradition based on political animosity (extending to periodic war) as well as cultural conflict and kept alive by the conflict in Northern Ireland today.[5] And the Irish, while not manifesting a consistent belief in the racial difference of the English from themselves, have built an entire culture around celebrating their ethnic superiority over the English and their Empire. Through the course of this analysis, I will therefore have to draw distinctions between racism which is based on skin color and racism which is based on national identity (Irish/British). Both are at work in the text but nationalist racism is far stronger. When Fergus says to Jody that his enabling belief as an IRA terrorist is simply "you guys shouldn't be here," he is, despite Jody's Caribbean origin and colonial sympathies, privileging Jody's British identity because of Jody's actions as a soldier in Ireland: by choosing to help occupy Ireland, Jody is English (Jordan 1993, 198). Fergus does not choose to privilege Dil's British identity for the same reasons. First, Dil's sexual otherness, combined with her racial otherness, subjects her to an even more marginal position within British society than does Jody's racial difference (this is possible because Jody "hides" his sexual difference and does not attempt to perform another gender). Second, Dil's expressed revulsion for Jody's part in occupying Northern Ireland aligns her with Fergus' own hatred of the British. It is telling that in Fergus' eyes Dil does not overcome his racial hatred for the English but merely crosses over to an acceptable kind of hatred--his own. If Dil were a staunch Unionist, the love affair would never have gotten as far as the bedroom and the lurking penis. Although Jody does not feel so English as Fergus' statement makes him out to be, he too is forced to identify himself in opposition to the Irish people who alienate him so thoroughly and immediately with their racism, aimed primarily at his identity as soldier and then his race. And his role as prisoner of the IRA forces him to identify further against the Irish, leading to his discussion of the Irish "nature." Jody tells Fergus that he knows Fergus will eventually have to kill him; "it's not in your nature," he says, to let him go:

>   FERGUS: What do you know about my nature?
>   JODY: I'm talking about your people, not you.
>   FERGUS: What the fuck do you know about my people?
>   JODY: Only that you're all tough undeluded motherfuckers. And that it's not in your nature to let me go (188-189)

The important thing about this conversation is Jody's and Fergus' willingness to accept the idea of a general Irish nature, as opposed, one imagines, to other nations and their unique characters. Jody can even define that character to a certain extent, and Fergus accept it. In fact, they discuss race overtly once more, when Jody reflects on Irish racism and experiments with a little English racism of his own:

FERGUS: What the fuck were you doing here?
JODY: I got sent...It was a job. So I get sent to the only place in the world where they call you nigger to your face.
FERGUS: Shouldn't take it personally.
JODY (He imitates a Belfast accent): "Go back to your banana tree, nigger." No use telling them I came from Tottenham.
FERGUS: And you play cricket?
JODY: Best game in the world.
FERGUS: Ever seen hurling?
JODY: That game where a bunch of paddies whack sticks at each other?
FERGUS: Best game in the world.
JODY: Never. (191)

While Jody's reason for signing up reveals the difficulties of a black, Caribbean native in finding a good job in England, he still resorts to an, if perhaps playful, overtly racist English persona to counter the sting of the Irish racism Fergus has no problem with. Jody begins to call Fergus "Paddy" after this, until Fergus tells him his real name. And while this exchange of names helps to overcome some of the racial tensions between the two, Fergus still thinks of Jody primarily in terms of his British identity, despite Jody's reminiscences of his Antigua home. For Jody is still a British soldier, and that must be his primary identity to an IRA terrorist, even one with a kindly "nature."

So Fergus and Jody's sexual attraction is not only complicated by the racial differences--of nationality and then color--between them, but something actually much less intractable than those racial differences. It doesn't take long for Fergus to respond to Jody sexually, but Fergus never really learns to overcome his racial hatred of the British, be they black or white, straight or gay. For when Fergus goes to London, he becomes not only "Jimmy," his own choice of pseudonym, but also "Paddy," and "Mick," according to the racism of his English employers. When he flees Northern Ireland after Jody's accidental killing and the surprise attack by the British army forces that destroys the IRA hiding place, Fergus becomes an Irish laborer, working on a construction site in England--in short, the lowest of the low on the English social scale, lower even, perhaps, than the non-whites who work with him, since he represents the irritating Irish and provokes traditionally negative responses from his English bosses. When the owner of the house Fergus is helping build finds him mimicking cricket batting with his sledgehammer on the site, he reacts: "So Pat's a cricket fan, eh?" Fergus tells him his name is Jim, not Pat; "Jim, Pat, Mick, what the fuck. Long as you remember you're not at Lords" (213). He is even lower than his Cockney overseer. And the first thing Dil asks him, when he goes to the address he got from Jody, concerns his ethnicity, as she tries to guess his accent, mimicking it as she tells him it's "like treacle" (209). Her failure to guess Irish, perhaps indicative of her revulsion from the place and the topic, caused by the recent history of Jody's death there, not only further removes Fergus from his true ethnicity but also reinforces how negative its impact is in this English society. She guesses Scots instead and Fergus agrees. Dil is the first person in London who treats Fergus like he is a fully human being, and he takes on self-esteem from his involvement with her, getting a sense of how to cope in his hostile environment. She introduces him to Col, the bartender at the bar she used to go to with Jody, and Col too treats him like a person; so Dil creates a new world for Fergus and secures his place in it with her love. Fergus is dependent upon this black woman's authority over those in her world, her power to insure his acceptance. He can accept this because her world is not overtly hostile to his national identity. This is the crucial basis of his acceptance. There is a similarity here to the relationship between Rose and Moran; although it is Moran who initially provides the authority and acceptance for Rose, letting her enter his privileged world, eventually Rose provides the authority and safe space for Moran. In Jordan's text, Fergus seems to have less trouble than Moran does accepting this turn of events, but this is because Fergus can still see himself as protecting Dil--literally, from Jude and the IRA, and figuratively from Dil's "real" gender.

And Dil's acceptance of Fergus, who, even as a Scots would be a suspect outsider, not only re-values Fergus but herself. For by attaching herself to a man in a traditionally feminine way, Dil also carves a safe space for herself in a world that is hostile to her in three ways: because of her race, because of her gender, and because of her penis. Dil is able to make her life much safer when she is attached to a man, who takes care of her in return for sexual favors and, in the case of Dave, her current lover when she meets Fergus, money. This set-up can quickly become abusive, as Dave's violence shows. So Fergus, kind yet strong, and able to physically subdue Dave, is Dil's perfect man, and she rewards his enactment of the traditional male role by being a traditional woman--a reward she pointedly refuses Dave, as we see when she explains her rejection of him to Fergus: "What was that all about?" Fergus asks, after beating Dave up for Dil. "He wants me to perform for him," Dil answers. "Perform?" "You know," she says, implying that Fergus must know what kind of performance she is speaking of, since all men desire it--the performance of faithful, feminine, sexually available womanhood made manifest primarily through sexual acts/acting. Her room, the script tells us, has "an exaggerated femininity about everything in it" (222), and has a large vanity, with mirror and assorted cosmetics, placed prominently within. She constantly refers to herself as a girl and complains of the difficulties of a girl's life when she is on her own. And she constantly refers to Fergus' "gentlemanly" qualities, noting that they appeal to her. When they first meet at the bar:

DIL: Everybody wants something.
FERGUS: Not me.

DIL: Not you. How quaint. How old-fashioned and quaint. Isn't it, Col?
...You old-fashioned?
FERGUS: Must be. (216)

When Fergus asks after Jody, and says he believes Dil misses him, she says, "dreamily," as the script specifies, "You say that like a gentleman...Like you're concerned...A real gentleman..." She also confirms that Jody "[is] a gentleman too" (225, 228). And she cements her monogamous devotion to Fergus after he tells her he wants to look after her, just as Jody did, and, to her mind, still does (226, 228).

Thus Dil's performance of the little woman not only makes a safe space for herself as a more threatened type of woman, but it also makes a safer space for Fergus. First, Dil's performance is ingenious because it relies upon traditional male essentialism for its success. She out-womans the average woman, completely engaging the patriarchal expectations of women, and thus cannot be attacked by men because, body parts aside, she is the essential woman. In this way, again, she is much like Rose Moran: playing along with the system makes her an instrument of change which can't be counterracted because it is being demanded by the very system it is changing. Dil plays on male essentialist gender demands to allow herself space to subvert them.

Second, the effectiveness of this heterosexual-seeming relationship in building Fergus' racial self-esteem is seen when he is visited by Dil at his work-site. This occurs after he has rejected her for her penis, yet his desire to disassociate himself from Dil is not stronger than his desire to protect her by associating with her--namely, to defend her as his "girl:"

DEVEROUX: Is that his tart? Does Pat have a tart?
FERGUS: She's not a tart.
DEVEROUX: No, of course not, she's a lady.
FERGUS: She's not that either...
[Dil] is acting bright and businesslike, like any wife...She pecks him on the cheek....
DEVEROUX: Do it on your own time, Paddy.
FERGUS: What?
DEVEROUX: Whatever it is she does for you.
Fergus looks from Dil to Deveroux.
FERGUS: If I was her I'd consider that an insult.
DEVEROUX: Consider it how you like. Just get that bloody tart out of here.

The private performer

Fergus stands up suddenly. He speaks quietly.
FERGUS: Did you ever pick your teeth up with broken fingers? ...It's a simple question.
Deveroux says nothing. Fergus looks down to Dil.
FERGUS: Come on, dear.
He holds out his arm. Dil gathers up her things and takes it. Her face is wreathed in a smile.
DIL: He didn't answer, honey--
Fergus walks her down the scaffolding ramp.
DIL: My, oh my, Jimmy, how gallant.
FERGUS: Shut up.
DIL: Made me feel all funny inside.
FERGUS: I said stop it. (235-236)

I relay this exchange at length because it shows how Fergus eventually sides with Dil against the racial hostility Deveroux uses to reduce them both to the lowest level--Fergus becoming Pat, Dil becoming Pat's tart. It is perhaps his regret over his own actions that make Fergus lash out at Deveroux; at any rate, his chivalry is re-engaged and Fergus goes back into the empowering role of Man that empowers Dil as His Woman, and both are freed from Deveroux's racism, which would reduce them to the lowest class of human being. Again, they become, at Fergus' and, ironically, Deveroux's command, the essential straight couple. One finds Fergus' re-assumption of chivalry to be the inevitable result of being forced to choose between what he considers two evils: giving up straightforward heterosexuality; or giving up racial hatred. If Fergus does not defend Dil from Deveroux's racism, he is acquiescing to it, reducing himself to Pat and Dil to Pat's tart. And this he cannot do, even if defending Dil means accepting a confounded sexuality, for that sexuality is, to Fergus, immediately the lesser of the two evils. Again the sexuality gap is bridged and the racial gap widened.

Of course, Dil's "reworkings of feminization," as Butler defines it, in "Gender is Burning," her discussion of Jennie Livingston's *Paris Is Burning*: is crucial in lessening the evil of that confounded (as Fergus sees it) sexuality. Dil's performance of femininity is her weapon, as noted above, against a hostile society:

> The performance is thus a kind of talking back, one that remains largely constrained by the terms of the original assailment: If a white homophobic hegemony considers the black drag...queen to be a woman, that woman, constituted already by that hegemony, will become the occasion for the

rearticulation of its terms; embodying the excess of that production, the queen will out-woman women, and in the process confuse and seduce an audience whose gaze must to some degree be structured through those hegemonies... (Butler 1993, 132)

Although Fergus is trying to convince himself Dil is not female, her successful "out-womaning of women" prevents him from doing so; he is indeed seduced by the hegemony of woman he sets up and participates in with Dil. Fergus cannot "see" Dil as a man, for if he claims her as his woman, she cannot be a man; he also sees her as British only in the most peripheral of senses--her (potentially negative) national identity is negated by her overwhelmingly (positive) femininity because his difficulties with her sexuality do not outweigh his racial hatred.[6] Thus the most womanly woman is at once marked by race yet risen above it, by virtue of her excessive identification with gender--in other words, she attains an honorary Irishness/otherness to match her honorary femaleness. This special status enables her to continue to uplift her man, Fergus, from his denigrating position of lower-class Irish laborer.

Jordan refers obliquely to this uplifting purpose in Dil's and Fergus' as well as and indeed because of Fergus' and Jody's relationship; in his introduction to the screenplay of *The Crying Game*, he states: "Underlying this friendship [between Jody and Fergus] lay an erotic possibility, a sense of mutual need and identification that could have provided salvation for their protagonists" (Jordan, 1993, xii). I read "could have provided salvation" as noting that the racism between Jody and Fergus remains unresolved; their friendship, even if erotic, cannot redeem them from the self-hatred both are tempted to engage in because of their unwilling/unwitting involvement in murderous politics. Because this relationship between men "tragically" fails, it must be taken up again by Dil and Fergus, in Jody's name.

Into this narrative of mutual empowerment through sexual compromise comes Jude. She represents the ultra-nationalist, non-feminine woman, and forces Fergus to again privilege his racial/national role (terrorist) over his sexual role (contented, fairly traditional domestic man). Jude rejects traditional masculinity--and with good reason, as the traditional men in the IRA never treated her with anything but contempt because of her sex. Content to ask her to allow a stranger to fondle her sexually in order to further his own

The private performer   97

plans, Peter Maguire then dismisses Jude's every attempt to play an intellectual role in the IRA, and the only words we hear him address to her are "Shut the fuck up, Jude." Jude predicted Fergus' refusal to kill Jody, but she is unrewarded for her insight. Now she is in London to teach Fergus that she is no weak woman but his boss from now on. She has dyed her hair dark brown, and says "Aye, I was sick of being blond. Needed a tougher look, if you know what I mean" (239). She rejects all that Dil is at pains to maintain, for it has gotten her nowhere. Rather than being rewarded for her femininity with a man's devotion, Jude has only ever received scorn. Now, although it is not her main preoccupation, Jude enjoys the power she obtains by plunging into the role of the zealous, partially-masculinized nationalist. She is in this way overcome by a negative male essentialism, for, unlike Dil, Jude sacrifices her feminine performance, her resistance, in order to take on unsubverted male power--evidenced most clearly by her gun. The gun, rather than any female identity, is her weapon. And Jude doesn't end up subverting male power because she is its pawn. She makes no safe space for her feminine performance. Instead, she gives up performance to become the essence of a killer--in short, masculine.

Jude is perceptive. And she brings race into the picture, as she informs Fergus of his obligations to the firm:

> JUDE: We've got some plans to execute here. And we'll need a Mister Nobody to execute them.
> FERGUS: No way, Jude. I'm out.
> JUDE: You're never out, Fergus...Maybe you don't care whether you die or not. But consider the girl, Fergus. The wee black chick.
> He leaps up from the bed.
> FERGUS: Leave her out of this.
> JUDE: Jesus, Fergus, you're a walking cliché. You know we won't leave her out of this. But I'm glad to see you care...And I must admit I'm curious. (240)

Jude puts an uncomfortably objective finger directly on Fergus' relationship to Dil--it is cliché. Down to the leaping from up from his bed. It is telling that Jude's response to his masculine bullying is to pull a gun and put it in his mouth. She may be glad to see Fergus cares for the wee black chick, but she is not about to put herself in Dil's position. She will not perform essential femininity. Her hostility to Dil is thus made up of racial as well as gender tension. Watching

Jude--the woman who becomes a man--react to Dil--the man who becomes a woman--one feels Jude could almost become the abusive boyfriend Dave was. And Jude also brings racial tension back into the relationship by referring to Dil's color and inferring she is curious about how the black woman is in bed, and about what Fergus gets out of such a kinky set-up. Race, for Jude, includes considerations of skin color. Because of this, it cannot even enter her mind that Fergus might consider Dil "on their side." For Jude it is kinky at best, sickening at worst to see Fergus involved with a black woman. This is ironic, as the Irish are wont to remind the world that they have been deemed the "blacks of the British Isles" in the eyes of the English.[7] Jude's first hostile encounter with Dil is marked by racism; as she and Dil spar for possession of Fergus Jude comments, "A bit heavy on the powder, isn't she, Jimmy?" (243) Jude is attempting to destroy Dil's performance of acceptable woman, trying to "read" her choice of femininity:

> For 'reading' means taking someone down, exposing what fails to work at the level of appearance, insulting or deriding someone. For a performance to work, then, means that a reading is no longer possible, or that a reading, an interpretation, appears to be a kind of transparent seeing, where what appears and what it means coincide...when what appears and how it is 'read' diverge, the artifice of the performance can be read as artifice; the ideal splits off from its appropriation...the impossibility of reading means that the artifice works, the approximation of realness appears to be achieved... (Butler 1993, 129)

We can take it that Dil's makeup not only helps create her femaleness but also lightens her skin, as powder generally does. But Dil ends up the victor in this battle--she will not be read. Part of what may irk Jude about Dil's race is that she presumes Fergus is attracted to Dil because of her exoticism, while Fergus only kept with Jude because she was there, the only woman available. If this is so, Jude again suffers at the hands of her traditional man, and seeks to destroy him. When Peter Maguire assaults Fergus, Jude tells him, "Leave him alone, Peter. He's in love" (Jordan 1993, 245). Her bitterness is clear.

So the effect of Jude's and Peter's intrusion into Fergus' London life is to reinstate his national/racial otherness, which was being ameliorated through Dil's acceptance. The return of his IRA colleagues forces Fergus to become an Irishman once more, and an Irish patriot-terrorist to boot. Fergus was always racially opposed to the British, but it was becoming an attitude only; Jude's (especially) and Peter's advent in Fergus' existence re-introduces violent racial hatred into Fergus' new life.

Fergus has begun to create a world where he calls the shots concerning how he manifests and defends his Irish identity. It is not as though Fergus resists being identified as an Irishman by Jude and Peter; what he resists is being forced back into the IRA master narrative, which defines patriot as cold-blooded killer.

Jude can reveal the artifice of this distinction, forcing Fergus to accept carrying out an assassination, but her attempts to reveal Fergus' assimilation of Dil into his non-British margin as an artifice by focusing on Dil's blackness are destined to fail because skin color is not the basis of Fergus' racial judgments. Just as Jody is more British than black because he is an occupying soldier, so Dil is less British than black because she disavows the politics of colonial oppression. Therefore Fergus' potential problems with Dil's identity performance is more focused on her sexual identity than her non-national racial identity (her skin color).

As Jordan puts it, commenting on whether the "nice terrorist" and the "pretty transvestite could live happily ever after" despite Fergus' potential for resistance to both Dil's race and national identity, "True love isn't about desire. It's about moral responsibility."[8] Thus Fergus' "chivalry" becomes the "true love" both he and Dil seek, rather than the dismissive paternal cliché Jude observes. But it is clear that this true love would not exist were it not premised on Dil's honorary exemption from a British identity. Fergus feels a moral responsibility toward Dil because she becomes "one of his own," a situation she appears to accept, despite its inherent slur on Jody.

When Fergus reveals to Dil his involvement in the IRA and Jody's death the night before he is due to assassinate the government official, he reveals the full extent of the demands and responsibilities of his commitment to his race, as he perceives them. But Dil will not let him fulfill that commitment. She ties him to her bed and keeps him from doing the job. Dil cannot let Fergus go because she refuses to be disempowered by the male world of politics once again, as she was when Jody was shipped off to--and killed in--Northern Ireland. This time she will be truly empowered, and exert power over the man she needs. This time the white body is tied up and subdued by the black body, again in the name of national politics. Fergus is trapped, and Dil accomplishes her goal; he can never go back to Ireland now.

Her privileging of their sexual relationship over his racial identity does not so much as enrage Fergus as frighten him. He knows the consequences of putting national identity second to personal desire, and when Jude shows up to kill Fergus in repayment for his no-show, Fergus is not surprised. He is anxious to get Dil to safety, however, which reinforces his continuing identification with her.

When Jude appears to kill Fergus, Dil reacts to both the sexual and racial threat Jude represents. She confronts Jude not only because Jude considers herself more of a woman than Dil (Dil is black) but because Jude considers Fergus' value as a terrorist to be greater than his value as a lover:

JUDE: You sick bitch.
DIL: You was there, wasn't you? You used those tits and that ass to get him, didn't you?
Fergus screams from the bed...Dil shoots Jude in the throat, and she falls dead, covered in blood. Dil turns the gun on Fergus.
DIL: She was there, wasn't she?...And she used her tits and that cute little ass to get him, didn't she?...Tell me what she wore.
FERGUS: Can't remember...
Dil points the gun at him, squeezing on the trigger. Then she stops. (264-265)

Dil resents Jude for being the perfect white woman who is rewarded by society with attentive, loving men--like her Jody. Jude represents the ultimate whiteness of femininity which Dil must work against yet try to approximate (hence the powder). To think that Jody was tempted by white womanhood is to suspect he did not consider Dil to be as womanly as Jude, and much as Fergus can't allow the owner of his work-site to reduce him to a Pat, Dil cannot allow a "cute, little" white woman to reduce her to a black (or a man). What Dil does not know is that Jude is only outwardly the perfect woman; that Jude could never have gotten and kept Jody because Jude will not perform femininity and create that safe space for herself and her man. Jude's lack of a safe space is revealed when Dil kills her. Dil is empowered by her performance, Jude is disempowered (violently) by her inability to perform. Jude is nothing but a terrorist, by this point, and that is not a safe space.

Similarly, Fergus, as Jude's colleague and co-conspirator, is also transformed negatively into an Irish man who helped lead Dil's lover to his death, but only briefly. Fergus is too intricately linked to her own self-esteem for Dil to be able to tolerate this vision for long, and she does not shoot him. But she tries to kill herself, unable to support herself as her world crumbles. However, when Fergus takes the gun away and gets her out of the apartment, thus freeing her from her deed, he is reinstated in Dil's eyes as a gentleman--she can see herself in him as his loving wifely counterpart--and she finds the strength to go on. He is protecting her once more. Only Jody remains in his original configuration of racial enemy, when Fergus turns to Jody's picture and tells his smiling face, "You should have stayed at home" (266).

In the end, Dil and Fergus seem to be setting out to preserve their relationship despite their separation during Fergus' prison sentence. Despite the fact that he is in jail for being an Irish terrorist, Fergus does not feel distanced from Dil. In fact, he states he is doing time for her: she is now an honorary Irish terrorist herself, having her time done for her by a loyal stand-in. The sexual chivalry of the action is again foregrounded by Fergus' assumption of the racial solidarity motivating it. Throughout the story, as the major boundaries of human identity--class and gender--are revealed to be fragile and easily blurred, save for race. The otherness of national/racial identity remains so strong that its power to kill is left unmitigated. Fergus can refuse to accept a biological definition of sex but he does not refuse to carry out a political assassination against a racial other. I would reiterate that his uneasiness with Dil's blackness is cancelled out by his eventual acceptance of her sexuality. If Dil were a patriotic British woman, her sexual difference would not outweigh her national/racial inclusion identity. This stance is, as I suggested above, a potential safety net for Jordan's text. Blaspheming traditional understandings of nationalist racial hatred (the Irish-British hostilities) is potentially far more dangerous for a writer from Ireland or England than trespassing gender lines. Just when the sexual text becomes most shocking (Dil reveals her penis), the nationalist text re-inserts itself almost as if to re-orient the viewer (Jude appears in Fergus' room) as to whom to sympathize with. This political maneuvering may not be as evident to American audiences as it is to British or Irish audiences, but it does function as a normalizing factor generally. Just as McGahern embeds his dangerous women within orthodox patriarchal farms and villages, Jordan embeds his dangerous sexual text within orthodox political dogma which he does little to challenge. Perhaps this is a reasonable price to pay for the opportunity to reach a large audience with a message of acceptance of sexual difference. But one wonders whether such a move is an inevitable alignment with an even more virulent type of reductive politics.

Is Dil's safety in heterosexual devotion a reductive politics? Only if it is seen as natural; Dil's body construction is constantly working as knowledge that runs counter to a natural reading of her relationship with Jody and/or Fergus. Her safety in heterosexual union is so sharply defined only because of her basic difference. In other words, in traditional definition of the term, Dil is outside the possibility of heterosexual union with a man because she is not "really" a woman. Therefore every aspect of her association with Fergus is performative. In this way, it cannot be essentialized into an oppressed submission to patriarchy or approbation of the oppressive gender relations inherent in patriarchy. Dil subverts the essence of woman by being a woman. Again, we are reminded not only of Rose Moran but of Rene O'Shaughnessy and her transcendent performance of wife and mother. By embracing both in an almost ferociously positive way, she breaks all the rules of patriarchal marriage and subverts the essence of patriarchy, which is well-defined paternity. In this way, patriarchal essence finds its undoing in a performative acceptance; performative in that women decide how to respond as women--literally how to be women--and this agency is the antithesis of essentialism.

Notes

1. I explore this point further in my Conclusion, where the political ramifications of this type of resistance are discussed at greater length.

2. See Joseph O'Neill (May 6, 1990). O'Neill's summation of *Amongst Women*'s plot--"The girls and boys grow up and away, the father weakens, and then he dies and is buried. That is the story"--is typical of those who see nothing beyond the preservation of the family's personal memories of a bittersweet, difficult but ultimately lovable patriarch(y), and praise the book for just that lack of internal dynamic, which they read as an homage to simple storytelling about the good simple Irish country people, and none of the denial of subjects in which "modern" fiction typically indulges.

3. In my consideration of critical readings of *The Crying Game*, I limit myself to using only those which go beyond the re-telling of plot so

unfortunately prevalent in analyses of movies. This necessarily limits the number of texts referenced.

    4. I am using the text of *The Crying Game* found in *A Neil Jordan Reader*. New York: Vintage Books, 1993. I find the stage directions crucial to my reading of the text, and therefore rely more on the "written" story than the filmic elements, most of which revolve around Dil's physique/physical identity.

    5. Edmund Spenser's infamous sixteenth-century essay concerning the state of Ireland merely expressed what had long been felt by the ruling classes in England. Unfortunately, his ideas about the non-human nature of the Irish remained current--and acceptable--well into the twentieth century. See David Cairns and Shaun Richards (1988) for a very detailed account of the effects of this de-humanization the Irish and Anglo-Irish literature, especially Chapter 3: "An essentially feminine race."

    6. Butler 1993, 132. In this passage, Butler is talking about racial passing, related to the Nella Larsen's novel *Passing*, concerning a black woman who passes as white, eventually paying for her deception with her life when her racist husband discovers her blackness. The ease with which this discussion of racial passing coincides with my discussion of sexual passing demonstrates Butler's point, which is that the two are intertwined, along with class, as necessary parts of one another. Butler comments on the racist husband's denied knowledge that his wife is not white (he calls her "Nig," for one thing) and his desire for that "hated" other; that the basis of passing lies not so much in the person passing as in other's desirous perceptions of that person is illustrated in remarks by Jaye Davidson, the actor playing Dil: "I keep telling people that I thought I could [play a woman] because of other people's reaction to me when I've been completely normal [i.e., looking masculine] and I've walked across the road to get a pint of milk. I've worn a vest and T-shirt...And they've said, 'Yes, thank you luv.' Maybe I'm fooling myself, maybe it's some sort of defense mechanism, but it's always other people. What other people see, they are welcome to have" (Giles 1991, 59--his italics).

    7. See Cairns and Richards 1988, 48: "In the discourse of Celticism the positional superiority of the English was guaranteed by the strategic formations of philology and anthropology which inscribed the Irish as members of a second-order race in relation to...the English...the notion of the Irish as a race of covert blacks, became increasingly popular in the 1860s [in] iconographic productions, such as those of Punch...Simianization placed the English in only one possible relation to the Irish--domination." Hence there is justification of the Irish sense of actual racial identification with the African-

Americans involved in the civil rights movement in the United States, which is often ridiculed as obviously impossible.

8. See Lois Gould (January 9, 1993), 24. Gould's "article," structured and presented as a screenplay in which she plays a (almost the) major role, is not as critical a source as one might hope.

Chapter Five

Going through the change: poison in the well

> I walked calmly, but inside me was building
> an unreasonable joy...I knew I must keep it...a secret...
> --*The Dream of A Beast*

After the building years of the 1950s and 1960s, Anglo-Irish experimental fiction of the 1970s and 1980s began to address the less immediate effects, or, more fittingly perhaps, the consequences of the importance of female performativity in the contemporary nation. Ireland experienced an economic boom from the late sixties through the early eighties, and a sense of expansion into the cosmopolitan world of contemporary literature was felt by Anglo-Irish writers, who began to revive the more experimental forms usually relegated by Irish critics and writers alike to James Joyce and Flann O'Brien. Cliché though it may be that acknowledgment of the female results in revival of the experimental and non-traditional, nevertheless its brief involvement with modes of expression other than the relentlessly naturalistic benefited Anglo-Irish literature, not least in developing an increased openness to female writers themselves. In Neil Jordan's novel *The Dream of A Beast*, this genre finds one of its most compelling expressions. And in John McGahern's play *The Power of Darkness*, written before and then compulsively re-written after *Amongst Women*, the role of women are considered with a troubled foreboding absent from his previous works.[1]

Taking the unanticipated form: Conscious Feminization

> She saw the half-drawn shape...as some kind of beast.
> ... that was the obvious form for such a shape... but what kind of beast?
> --*The Dream of A Beast*

The narrator and, again, unnamed protagonist of Jordan's second novel confronts the reader with his transformation from average human to something else from the outset of his story.[2] "When I came to notice it," he says in the first sentence, "it must have been going on for some time" (Jordan 1983, 89). In keeping with the feeling of the title, these massive changes not only in his own body but in the earth itself are presented in a detailed yet strangely vague manner: one could sum it up bluntly, saying it is the story of apocalypse, as the earth (sited in Dublin) reverts/develops into a primeval rainforest jungle of strange and gigantic plants and a very few humans are metamorphosed along with it into non-human creatures which nevertheless retain the ability to think, feel and reason in human ways. The narrator is the first to so change, and is forced to abandon human ways and places, including his wife, child, home and job. At the end of the novel, the apocalypse is complete and those few creatures left alive converge peacefully by an ancient seashore to await whatever future there may be. The very end is ambiguous, leaving open the possibility, not necessarily comforting, that the whole story was indeed just a dream; the narrator is reunited with his wife Marianne, who is also a beast: "The kiss was long, long enough for the sun to cross the dial, for the moon to traverse it and for the sun to rise once more. I saw the globes of her eyes and in my visage reflected there saw something as human as surprise" (175).

That is the bare outline of the story and its surface riddle. I quote the final lines because their compression of time, so apparently dreamlike, and their concluding feeling of waking, and surprise to see that what one has dreamt of is not real, offer the possibility that the narrator's transformation is imaginary. This offer is not simple, not simplifying, not reductive, but, on the contrary, a complicating maneuver in a story which prefigures in more ways than one Jordan's concern with the portentous appearances and realities of femininity. Jordan has referred to *The Dream of A Beast* as a novel that really should have been and was trying to become a screenplay; and indeed there are pages which hold only a handful of lines, chapters which consist of one page, the result of Jordan's desire to show more and more evocatively, through brief word pictures, the images he feels are hindered by telling.[3]

This novel, which has been generally invisible to critics, is not merely the product of literary experimentation, not an indiscriminate fantasy about an inability to cope with modern urban life, not a throwaway marking the difficult transition to film. Rather, it is a crucial consolidation of the key elements of Jordan's work, for in it one sees his growing realization that the appearance of the body is just one manifestation of the desires of the mind, and in realizing this connection he erases the difference between intellectual desire and physical reality/appearance. This is obviously the framework plot structure of *The Crying Game*, *The Miracle*, *Angel*, and, to a certain extent, *Mona Lisa*.[4] It is not a question of simply willing oneself to be what one desires to be, but more like an inability to stave off coming to resemble and gradually, irrevocably, to be what one actually is.

In *The Dream of A Beast*, the protagonist/narrator is an average man--a husband, father, business colleague, suburban neighbor. But from the beginning of his story what he notes is his subtle difference from that male norm:

> But then I've always been a little simpler than those around me. By that I mean that people somehow, even friends of mine--perhaps mostly friends of mine--would find plenty of chances to laugh at me...Things they seemed to take for granted I found difficult, and vice-versa. Tax-forms, for instance, I could never fill out properly, so I would put them off until the writs began to arrive...I often wondered: had my eyes been given a different focus to most others, so that while we looked at the same scene all right we saw quite different things? And of course people laughed, they will laugh, even get indignant, as when the tea you make is weak or you burn the toast only on the one side. (90)

This is the first of many observations the narrator makes of his own difference from other average people which ultimately hinges on his ultra-sensitivity to detail and the natural world and his uselessness with the tools of civilization. He describes it here at the first as being "simpler" than others, but what he inevitably describes as his unusual characteristics are traditionally feminine traits. He is good at drawing, creating images in his mind, he is good with children, he loves to play the piano, he is sensitive and vulnerable to the tactile impressions of scents, textures, and animals. He is no good at math, does not attend to the non-creative side of his business, and cannot impose his will on his wife, Marianne. He is, to Marianne and their friends, passive, creative, dithery--stereotypically female.

I posit that it is this realization of himself as being a man with a traditionally feminine being which precipitates the male narrator into his sensations of being transformed into a non-human beast. In this way, the narrator is much like Dil in *The Crying Game*; both are de-humanized (in the eyes of others) by a dual nature and the prominence of the feminine within it, and both seek the understanding of a traditional partner to help them through this crisis of identity. And both find their bodies the focal point of controversy. In Dil's case, her body is offered as a sacrifice to the IRA (when Fergus cuts her hair and dresses her as a man), but the sacrifice of identity is temporary. In the case of the beast, his body is offered up as a sacrifice to human nature, and the loss, corresponding to the end of the world and the human race, is permanent. Gender blurring invites the apocalypse.

The beast cannot occupy the safe space Dil occupies as a woman because he cannot perform, even outwardly, one gender or the other. He cannot "pass" as male or female because he is irretrievably both, and this is potentially the most de-humanizing state of being according to the rules of his society. It is as if the narrator represents the worst-case (as his society sees it) result of the feminine performance that undermines the solid base of masculine solidarity. Gradually understanding himself ill-fitted to play out his masculine role, the narrator cannot imagine playing any other role which would not be completely unnatural. In this way, his struggle to find a workable identity is an analogy for patriarchal Irish culture in general as it struggles to redefine its bases of authority in the face of long-term, below-the-surface feminine/feminist challenges. The narrator's dilemma takes on national significance in this context, as the pressure of keeping his internal feminization from changing his outward body manifests itself in his body's rapid alienation from the human norm itself. As he can no longer be a traditional man, he is not allowed to become a woman, he is forced to go outside the (two) traditional human forms and become something neither male nor female. So he becomes a beast.[5]

All of his descriptions of his change draw on women and the feminine. The physical changes from human male to indeterminate creature halt temporarily when he makes love to Marianne. His dream after this lovemaking is the first of a series of the dreams of the beast which allude to his appropriation by women. These dreams of women are extremely exotic: in one of Jordan's comments on the book he alludes to "a certain thing about the dreams of animals that people have" (Hansen 1991, 41). Is the narrator the animal whose dreams are being delineated for people, or is the narrator dreaming of women as exotic animals, the kind he wishes he could become? He dreams of a room full of women whom he watches from above, lying on a plate glass ceiling: "each woman carried a cup...[glistening] with liquid. They entered a tiny arch and came out again with each cup empty...they all pressed into a circle and stared at me together...the glass below me melted and they each held a cup up to gather the drops. I melted in turn and an arm gathered me in a raised cup and a woman's face with two soft, feathered lips bent towards me to drink" (Jordan 1983, 97). When the women uncover his surveillance, their gaze melts him, and he is consumed by them, literally melted down and re-cast into the body of a woman. When he awakes, he compares his skin to that of Marianne's and finds his unutterably coarse in comparison; his physical masculinity is becoming repellent to him compared to the "softness" and "whiteness" of the women.

But for all the uncertainty at home and the discomfort with his body, as he walks to work the narrator feels what he calls joy at his sense of irretrievable changes overtaking human society. "This joy was nameless...but I found if I gave my thoughts to it it answered back...It frothed inside me...My tough nails scraped off my forehead...The joy abated then and became still water. I knew I must keep it as much a secret as my monstrous hands" (100). If his body must mutate, surely the companion mutation of the earth into a jungle of gargantuan flowers and roots is a comforting sign that there is a place for a being which can be neither fully male nor fully female and hence, by human standards, a being which cannot be fully human. Another standard is emerging, another environment, in which the narrator is acceptable, indeed, perhaps, desirable.

His task at work is to design an ad for a musk perfume, and his drawing reflects, and helps to create, his new state: a woman in a bathtub, only her leg showing, threatened by an unknown entity in the foreground which becomes the narrator in his non-human form. As the drawing progresses the creature becomes more majestic than threatening, a counterpart to the unseen woman, whose ignorance of his presence begins to seem more a lack of concern. This is the relationship the narrator has with the woman who brings him the musk account; also unnamed, she is immediately attractive to the narrator, despite beauty irregularities like a cracked front tooth. She tells him her life story when they meet, and he has another dream after she finishes telling him:

> Her odalisque eyes were wide open on mine all the time she spoke. They were by no means beautiful, but they gripped me. I fell into the dream again, with the daylight all around me, I saw a long, golden stretch of desert...My eyes sped over these stretches, the outlines hardly varying till the expanse was broken by a jagged rectangular shape, pure black, sinking at some angle into the sand...Inside I could glimpse a face...hair frozen in statuesque, perpetual disarray. I had never seen the face before. One of the teeth was cracked. (104)

The face he sees is hers, and his own. She is, in fact, his female self, the actual woman he might have been. After he meets her he feels "the rush of joy" again (105), but again must hide it and his new body on the train home: "Knowing how each one of us assumes that what is seen of him by others is not what he knows to be the truth but a mask, I felt a sudden terror that the whole of me was about to be laid bare" (107). He has by this point gone beyond masking his feminization to masking his non-humanity itself.

At this point, he again meets a woman--his mother is on the train, and he dreams of his childhood. Again, as with Marianne, when he looks at his mother's human, female body, his own seems grotesque in comparison; he remembers counting freckles on her arm and his own arm mutates in "a sudden surge" (109), ripping out his shirtsleeve. But he must soon give up the company of women to focus on the advertising agent, who becomes his lover. She alone can see what is happening to him, she is not repelled by his transformation because she is somehow spiritually kin to him. Marianne can see what is happening, but she is repelled by it.

Here Jordan's text becomes mercurially slippery as it offers varying readings: Marianne is repelled by her husband's femininity; Marianne is repelled because her husband has actually become a non-human creature; Marianne is oblivious to her husband but he imagines his own strong feelings of self-disgust are readily apparent to her and blames them for her decision to throw him out; Marianne does not throw him out at all--he chooses to leave because he cannot deal with her successful femininity and projects his feelings onto her. One is offered at all times the possibility that the narrator is not really physically mutating, that the physical change is a metaphor for his recognition of his femininity--his constant daydreaming and the dream-like distortion of his encounters keep alive the possibility that one is merely taking part in his dream and that all will return to normal once he wakes up. But one is also offered at all times the possibility that the narrator really is physically mutating, and that feminization is a metaphor for d/evolving into a beast. Finally choosing between these two options, however, is never demanded. It is not the point. The point is the confusion of all norms, the uselessness of all signposts, which is the result of blurring the barrier between genders.[6]

While at home, the narrator dreams again of women. The most telling is his first dream, that he is suspended by a rope and is trying to swing over and catch hold of a perfect female leg, but the leg "walked off abruptly, as if its owner was tired of waiting" (116). The implications are clear, as the narrator seeks his perfect feminine form but finds that form claimed by its true "owner," a real female. He cannot be a woman, and this unhappy realization spurs and completes his change into a completely non-human beast. "Woman and the world that word implied seemed as strange a bestiary to me as the world I had become," he states, and manages eventually to find some acceptance of this fact, that it is too late to stop his change into something beyond man or woman (128).

When the narrator leaves his home forever, he flees to the abandoned city center, now a wilderness, to live in a joyous seclusion. When he meets his lover, she tells of her girlhood, stories of which he never tires, as he is hearing what his life as a woman might have been like. Now, he says, his dreams are of humans (141). He dreams of himself as a typical man, and finds this image of himself "absolutely unfamiliar" (141). He dreams this man meets Matilde, the narrator's child, as a grown woman, and he is amazed at the vision of this woman he has managed to produce out of his maleness. But his dreams are interrupted by a young boy who discovers the narrator's hiding place in the city and befriends him. For a time he, the boy, and the woman live happily together. The beast and the woman discuss the laws of life: "Does not one law rule us all? I asked her. How can it, she answered, or else we would have seen it...If there were, she asked me, would you obey it?...law, if law there was, revealed itself in retrospect, like a sad bride coming to her wedding too late to partake in it" (153-154). The beast eventually moves beyond even those laws the woman can abide by, and when she sees that he has moved beyond gender itself, she leaves him in terror.

Again, the same questions that pertain to Marianne's ejection of the narrator apply here: does the lover reject a beast or a feminized man? or does a man reject the woman he wants to be, not just have? Whichever reading one takes, the problem is that the woman is bound by human/gender law, and this difference from the narrator drives her from him. The narrator's next companion, a bat named Alarth, tells him that loathing has been the narrator's companion "for some time," and helps him to free himself from the memory of those human women whom the narrator has been comparing himself unfavorably to for so long (157). Thus freed from human law, the narrator, who can now fly, later finds his former lover working as a prostitute and discovers that she is beginning to change into a beast too; she says she is inexplicably glad (169).

The conclusion of the story finds the world uninhabitable for humans, and the boy, dying, is subsumed into the body of the narrator. He thus fulfills the function of a kind of pregnancy and life-giving, though this child will never leave his body. The narrator/boy meets a few other beasts, among them Marianne, who has subsumed the dying Matilde into herself. "The boy inside me leapt," says the narrator, managing at last to combine both male (boy), female (his pregnancy), and the non-human (his beastliness). And while hers is unexplained, Marianne has also suffered or celebrated a change which makes her beastly (though she is not masculinzed) "If things lead us to anything, [Marianne] said to me, they surely lead us to realisation" (174). At these words, they come across a signpost reading HOPE ETERNAL, and as they kiss, the narrator concludes with his final beast's dream, of waking to find himself human in her eyes.

Again, the question is not really whether the transformation was just a dream; whether a human male actually turns into a monster or just feels/comes across as one as a result of his feminization is not the point. It is the feminization itself, and its categorization as monstrous that is examined in the story, and that cannot be explained away as fantasy or dream. Jordan's fantastical tale is then a mirror held to the very real fears of Ireland's patriarchal consciousness as it seeks to address the very real changes being worked upon it by that strange and powerful force of the feminine.

Dramatic Crudities: The End of the Farm

> You women are terrible.
> --*The Power of Darkness*

In John McGahern's first stage play, *The Power of Darkness*, the family-run, rurally-isolated, tyrannical and tyrant-making Irish farm is again central to the story of a young man who sees himself driven to murder and marriage by his mother and mistress. But this time, the farm does not stand aloof from and unchanged by the violent actions of its dwellers; this time, the farm itself is destroyed-- something McGahern seems, at long last, to see as perhaps a positive thing. In his introduction to the play, he delivers an unusually concise and damning eulogy for the rural family community he has developed with such complexity and love-hate feelings in his previous works:

> *The Power of Darkness* is a perfect description of that heart [of Irish society] and is uncannily close to the moral climate in which I grew up. The old fear of famine was confused with terror of damnation. The confusion and guilt and plain ignorance that surrounded sex turned men and women into exploiters and adversaries.
> Amid all this, the sad lusting after respectability, sugar-coated with sanctimoniousness and held together by a thin binding of religious doctrine and ceremony, combined to form a very dark and explosive force that, generally, went inwards and hid. For anybody who might imagine this to be a description of a remote and dark age, I refer them to the findings of the Kerry Babies Tribunal in 1985. It is in the nature of things that such a climate also creates the dramatic hope, or even necessity, of redemption. (McGahern 1991, vii)

I find McGahern's reference to the Kerry Babies case as a powerful example of the "dark ages" climate in Ireland telling.[7] The instance of a young unmarried woman persecuted by the police for murdering her infant has echoes within McGahern's text, which focuses on the evil deeds of women who are forced into that evil by the vindictiveness of their men--fathers, lovers, husbands, and sons--and the social consequences of this vicious circle.

Paul is a weak, vain young man hired on to help with the horses on Peter King's rich farm and stables. He is in every way from start to finish completely determined by his relationships to women: he is bullied and coddled by his mother Baby into taking the job; he may have to leave the job because he gets a young woman, Rosie, pregnant; he stays because Eileen King wants to marry him; his marriage to Eileen fails because of his affair with Maggie King, Eileen's step-daughter; he betrays his wife's and mother's murder of Peter King because his grief and guilt at having to bury Maggie's and his aborted child on Maggie's wedding night lead him to believe he must sacrifice himself and the women to justice.

While it is true that Eileen King, Baby, and Maggie King bend the somewhat slow-witted Paul to their will, what McGahern's text is at pains to demonstrate is Paul's willingness to depend upon the women for guidance, his utter refusal to take responsibility for his own actions and, inevitably, his and their downfall. He often addresses his constant refrains of disavowal to "You--" or "those women:" "Once a man gets mixed up with women he never knows whether he's coming or going. He'd be far better to go out into the fields and eat grass with the horses" (14); "You women have everything through other [confused]. I don't know whether I'm coming or going" (23-24); "There's no holding back these women once they start to turn wicked" (35); "Being with these women when they get riz is like being in with the devils in hell" (37); "You women drive a man round in circles" (41); etcetera. Paul is completely amoral, willing to be led into the actions he wants to take but too weak-willed to carry out on his own. But his society provides, in the form of women, his escape route from and scapegoat for the bad fruits of his complicity.

When he abandons the pregnant Rosie, dooming her, he is lordly in his dismissal--"She has to be shown the door. I'll soon give her the message"--but when his life is in a shambles because he chooses Eileen, he blames Rosie herself--"Rosie, oh Rosie, why didn't you keep me? It was my one chance. You should never have let me go" (13, 46). When he helps his mother Baby and Eileen King get away with finishing off the ailing Peter King before Peter gives the farm to his sister, Paul claims over and over that he wants no part of "a poor man's money;" once he is married to Eileen he revels in that ill-gotten wealth, and then, predictably, when it goes sour he blames Eileen—"...I couldn't turn in the place but Eileen was there...I didn't know then that she gave him the poison. I was never able to touch her after she told me she gave him the poison" (46). Finally, when Paul's and Maggie's illegitimate child is aborted and he is forced to bury it lest Maggie's new husband finds it, he records his own complicity but blames his mother, Eileen and Maggie herself under the rubric of "you women": "I wouldn't have done anything if [Maggie]'d said even a word....Why have you done this to me, Mother?...How did I get into the hands of such a pair of devils out of hell?" (46, 47).

It is not surprising, given Paul's habitual relegation of guilt to the women, that it is at the urging of his father Oliver that he decides not to kill himself, thus paying the ultimate price for murder and deception, but to reveal to the wedding crowd in the house Eileen's and Baby's murder of Peter King and Maggie's aborted pregnancy in a sort of reverse-confession. As he names each woman he's wronged, he ultimately ruins her life by revealing her "sin." He tells about getting Rose (who is now married) pregnant, murdering Maggie's father and getting her pregnant as well as helping conceal the abortion, implicating Eileen and Baby in both the murder and the abortion. Thus clearing his conscience, Paul not only delivers himself up to the angry crowd at Maggie's wedding but, of course, also turns in the women. "General mayhem" ensues (51-52). Paddy, the drunken stableman, sums up Paul's actions--"You're a poor fool, Paul. You'll never get that in your head"--in a cold counterpoint to Oliver's and Paul's otherworldly religious fervor (52).

Paul's uselessness in a world seemingly run by "those women" is matched by his father Oliver's passive, pathetic retreat into religious platitude in the face of his wife Baby's steamroller practicality and force of will. Paddy too is a weak, insubstantial old man dependent upon Eileen King for his livelihood and well-being. Peter King was once strong and demanding, but his illness puts him in the power of Eileen and Baby and it is during a typical rant against Eileen's intractability that Peter is finished off by his long-suffering wife and interested neighbor.

So the men in the story are rendered marginal by the women. Paul, Oliver, and Paddy are stereotypically "feminized," weak and indecisive. Peter King is deposed by his queen after his struggle to retain power reveals the extent to which he depends upon his woman to maintain his pride of place in the house. It is as if one were visiting the Moran farm at Great Meadow thirty years later and finding the descendants of those empowered daughters devolved completely into evil. Here McGahern re-produces the stock characters of his family-farm fiction, only this time gone horribly wrong, turned into grim parodies of their former natures. And this time, the story is set in the present rather than the iconic Dark Ages-1950s; above, McGahern insists upon the currentness of the story. What is the importance of siting this play in the present?

Perhaps an answer to this question lies the sense one has when reading *The Power of Darkness* that one is viewing the fruits of the family relations in *Amongst Women*, *The Pornographer*, and *The Dark*. The struggles of women against co-optation into patriarchy, the undercutting of patriarchal structures by various female performances of family itself which are presented as just beginning to take effect in these earlier stories, are now shown to have effected a fundamental change upon the rural, patriarchal family--and, by extension, contemporary Irish society itself. In this way, *The Power of Darkness* is the most symbolic of McGahern's texts, because it seeks to portray gender relations without the richness of prose fiction, replete with description and explanation. Stripped down, the relations between the sexes appear at their most stark--and their most negative. Everyone speaks for themselves, and the selves they speak for are bleak.

Is this, then, at last an indictment of the women who infiltrated and deflated the patriarchal structures they inherited? A rueful condemnation of the female performance of reality and modernity which McGahern had applauded at its auspicious outset? For the female characters indict themselves often enough, with exhortations to cold-bloodedness in the name of practicality. But here the text develops perhaps the most complexity of any McGahern text, as it forces the reader to recognize a dense system of relationships and motives rather than rest at the level of morality play. McGahern resists the usual commentary on feminism gone awry provided by the resurgent conservatism of the 1980s and presents, instead, a study of patriarchal failure which firmly implicates the masculine.

First, Peter King's role, so similar to Moran's and Old Mahoney's, is patently outdated by the text. His insistence on running his farm on a nineteenth-century budget with similarly Victorian roles for his family and hired help are presented in no uncertain terms in the Notes on Characters: "He expects [Maggie and Eileen] to work like servants, and he does not allow his money to spread ease or comfort" (ix). He only hires Paul when he is too ill to work himself, and chooses Paul because Paul's family owe King money; Paul thus works to pay off the debt and receives no wages. Paddy, a World War II veteran, lives in the past and in his alcoholism-cum-wit characterization fulfills the tired role of the drunken Irish comedy relief. Paul is the handsome, silly, vain, superstitious, childish romancer right out of *The Playboy of the Western World.* Oliver is the laughable religious ascetic who pontificates without any effect and whose tag lines might have come from *The Poor Mouth.*

These men, each potentially able to command respect and influence in their own spheres, are reduced to nuisances by their own rigid adherence to outdated social roles. They do not allow for any change in society, and expect to be able to live in much the same way as their fathers--accountable to no one but themselves by virtue of their money (King), their position as father (Oliver and King), their handsome youth (Paul), and/or their handicaps (Paddy). They are stereotypical Irish men. And they wish to return the farm and its family society to the colonial era, when a man was master of his home because he was master of nothing else; a time when there was no law for Irishmen but their own will. When the nation was new (the 1930s-1950s), law was made by other Irish men, and householders like Michael Moran could exist comfortably enough to allow their wives to thwart their will from time to time. Now the laws of the nation seem to be made by strangers (young people and women), and the men of the house are self-righteous in their rejection of the new oppression. This rejection of an aggregate, representative social authority in favor of the word of the master is an attempt to restore the colonial authority of the patriarch.

The men of this contemporary farm do not even cherish the household, as Moran and even as the narrator of *The Pornographer* comes to cherish it, as a material representation of their own lives and love of the earth. Peter King does not love his farm. To him it is a place of business and his family live there as other families live above their shops. The only permanence is the income from the land, and it is the most important thing. This materialist outlook helps revert the farm to colonial days, when the land was money for the landowner (Peter) and a site/source of miserable poverty for those who worked it for him (Eileen and Maggie).

The fact that Ireland has no healthy place left for traditional Irish masculinity is indicated by the effect of the men's intractable gender role-playing on the women. The women, Baby, Eileen, Rosie, and Maggie, are still bound to men by custom, law, and, therefore, necessity. This is the first problem with the society these men maintain. Because the women are still forced to marry in order to survive in their society, they have no bonds other than legal to their men. Baby's cold-bloodedness when dealing with her husband Oliver, son Paul and neighbor Peter King is but the logical outcome of a society which refuses to allow her to stand on her own. Baby rids herself of her husband's interference in her actions by encouraging his otherworldliness, which then gives her good reason to ignore him. The Notes describe Oliver as a "decent" man, but there is no sympathy for his sort of decency, which is predicated on unreflective submission to religious law. She subdues Paul by exerting on him the force of her inarguable intelligence--she always thinks things out two steps ahead of him, then manipulates him by confronting him with the ridiculous naïveté of his own ideas. Peter King's death leads to her son's marriage to Eileen King and Baby's own subsequent enrichment, so Peter King, too, is overcome.

Baby is obviously intelligent, but her position as a woman in a society which won't let go of past gender hierarchies reduces her to someone who is, as the Notes put it, "oily and worldly-wise" (ix). She must be oily, for it is only by selectively greasing the rusty wheels of her husband's and son's minds that she can accomplish anything for herself. "She is perfectly in tune with her circumstances," say the Notes; an unfortunately true statement (ix). Baby is in tune with the village world and knows exactly how to placate it through appearances (Wife, Mother) while going behind its back to get what she wants. Her method, however, is completely different from Rose Moran's or Una O'Shaughnessy's, for it eschews these older women's respect for the system they wish to enter and help manipulate. As noted above, the profit-oriented outlook of the men concerning the farm has affected the women as well, who simply want a hand in the profits. This is far from Rose's pride in the farm and the household, as well as from Una's pride in her husband or Rene's mystical enriching of her men through her augmentation and love of the family structure. Baby's and Eileen's and Maggie's men do not ask them to enrich them spiritually, and these women have therefore come to deride the very existence of the spiritual.

Eileen King also fulfills her role as Wife to Peter and partial Mother to Maggie King. We learn that Eileen is half Peter's age, hired on as it were to labor on the farm as unpaid help. She is granted none of the comforts or respect due a wife but is still expected to perform all the duties of a wife--and then some. She is finally induced to kill Peter when she learns that, in his dying hour, he has sent for his sister in order to leave the farm to her instead of Eileen, which would effectively turn Eileen out of the house and onto the road. She is not as intelligent as Baby, but Eileen manages to get what she wants--marriage to the handsome Paul, whom she capably seduces. And she has the strength to keep her role in Peter's death a secret, as well as to get the interfering Maggie married off against her will.

Maggie King has been brought up in the shadow of her father to be blindly loyal to him. She hates Eileen and avenges herself and her father by seducing Paul and ruining Eileen's marriage, but is then destroyed herself when Paul gets her pregnant and she must choose to abort the baby before her prospective groom finds out. Baby "convinces" her to do it: "Baby soon told her what is what. People have a habit of coming to their senses when they are told what is what" (41). Maggie, recovering from the abortion on her wedding night, carries through with keeping the secret up until Paul's disastrous confession. She is foolish, but she knows "what is what"-- namely, that some lines cannot be crossed. "[You've] had your fun," as Eileen says; "Now you'll have to get rid of the fun" (41). All three women are bound to the law of the community which is the law of the Father; in this way, they are apparently no different than Rose, Una, the nurse, or any other Irish woman. But what the contemporary women crucially lack is the desire to subvert male law in the long run. They simply play for short-term stakes and are unable to see that the entire social system must be subverted in order to put an end to their suffering. These women have no resources to help them do otherwise; the farm itself was once the goal worth waiting for, and now it is stripped of its spiritual value, unable to contribute to anyone's self-esteem. So they fight violent battles while--almost because--they are relinquishing the fighting of the war.

And this is what, ultimately, the text decries. Each woman is presented as being offered no other choice than to transgress the usual moral law because her personal integrity is transgressed from the outset. Because each is demeaned as a woman, each cannot help but commit demeaning acts, or even, in the case of Baby, to set about deliberately demeaning the men who are supposed provide her a share in a superior (male) identity. She kills Peter King for the money he keeps lording over her, and Eileen bullies Paul into standing up against Oliver's desire that Paul marry Rosie only so Eileen can marry Paul and command him as Peter commanded her. Eileen bullies Maggie because she cannot stop the cycle of violence she is born into in which only one woman can be important in a household. For the same reason, Maggie seduces Paul to thwart Eileen, but ends up helping to corner herself into an unwanted marriage. Maggie is pressured into aborting her fetus and marrying out of the family because she cannot break the law which says the family reputation is more important than personal happiness. She and Rosie are both undone by this tenet, since it is Baby's denigration of Rosie's morals which leads to her banishment. Baby will not have another woman in the house; she cannot afford to. Women, in this anachronistic world, cannot show any sympathetic, humane feeling.

This is what the play brings home so forcefully. The amorality of the women is the direct result of the immorality of the men who keep them ensconced in an outdated, diseased social structure. The question is begged, at this point--does this hark back to Rose Moran, and her decision to participate in patriarchy, thereby undercutting it from inside, gradually, rather than to fight it, as the nurse in *The Pornographer* or even Una O'Shaughnessy chose to do? Questions about the efficacy of surface complicity with the patriarchal (Rose Moran, Renee O'Shaughnessy) as opposed to open war against it (Una, the nurse) seem woven into the fiber of *The Power of Darkness*. What is, after all, the darkness of the text's title? Is it stifling patriarchy, or the difficulty women face in maintaining consistent open attack on patriarchy? Rose Moran's story was one of maneuvering through the narrow pathways open to women within a patriarchal family structure; was she following an ultimately empowering path or only wending more deeply into the morass she might have cleared up from outside? Is Eileen King her descendant, or is it Baby, or, neither? Perhaps Rose Moran has no descendants in the present day--how then has her seemingly empowered undercutting of patriarchy been prevented from bearing fruit?

These may seem to be oddly dramatic questions, but McGahern calls for dramatic salvation at the outset of *The Power of Darkness*. He recounts the strange need that kept him returning and returning to the text, and how he finally devoted himself to it after, significantly, finishing *Amongst Women*. *The Power of Darkness* originated as an adaptation of Tolstoy into "Irish speech" for a BBC radio presentation. That play was finished and produced, yet McGahern kept "returning again and again" to the play, changing it, between his prose works. That he finally finished it in its present form after he completed *Amongst Women* suggests the influence the unfinished play had on the novel.[8]

The relation also suggests McGahern's concern that the "historical" society he was portraying was not, in fact, relegated to the mists of history. As he wrote other texts, set in the 1950s and 1960s, the story of *The Power of Darkness* was moving through them; when he turned to the play itself, it was set in the present. One might intuit a growing, if not nagging, realization on McGahern's part that he could not produce another text which seemed to resolve female performance by showing its encouraging beginnings and leaving its development to the unseen future. In this way, *The Power of Darkness* represents a crisis in McGahern's understanding of femininity and what it might take to reform Irish patriarchal society. He presents women who are grown strong by virtue of oppression, but reveals that strength to be of necessity inhuman. He presents men who are grown weak by virtue of stagnation, and reveals that weakness to be endemic and unchallenged by male law. This most uncertain and wary of his long works offers the most undilutedly negative commentary on a society whose patriarchal essence has perhaps proven more long-lived than he previously imagined.

McGahern participates in the move away from naturalistic realism even as his subject matter stays the same by representing societal ills in symbolic forms; the evil of the farm and those who live on it in *The Power of Darkness* seem animated by an almost cartoon-like violence and two-dimensional expression. The complex, undeniably contemporary emotions and blighted hopes at work in the characters do not find a vent in new, unusual ways. And in this way, McGahern chooses to remain outside the realm of fantasy but enters the realm of allegory. McGahern's future is just as uncertain as Jordan's, and by addressing this worrying uncertainty honestly and unflinchingly, McGahern remains politically relevant and important to a new generation of readers within and without Ireland.

While Jordan's later works seem to offer positive outlooks on the possibility of blurring gender hostility, he maintains his common link with McGahern, no matter how disparate their form and subject matter seem to be, and that link is the certainty that change can only come about through intensive, one-to-one personal relationships between men and women—whether or not one has to put "men" and/or "women" into qualifying quotes. Jordan does not focus on the family unit as specifically as McGahern, but his couples are exclusive and faithful to each other, creating the basis of good families. Interaction between these men and women may not be traditionally reproductive, but that is their saving grace.

Notes

    1. McGahern 1991. I will examine more fully below McGahern's self-described compulsion to write the play.
    2. Neil Jordan 1983, in *The Neil Jordan Reader*. All quotes will be taken from this edition.
    3. Marlaine Glicksman (January 1990). Commenting on how *The Dream of A Beast* and Robbe-Grillet "play with literary form," Jordan sayss. "That was one of the reasons I actually wanted to make films. Because...they allowed me to tell stories and operate with more operatic sweep than I could do in fiction...They [movies] gave me more freedom to explore things that I probably would never have done in fiction" (68).
    4. I have chosen not to focus on *Mona Lisa* because its themes of sexual disguise and supposed betrayal are, for my purposes, much more profitably complicated in *The Crying Game*.
    5. See Lewis Jones (January 7, 1984) for a hazily-glimpsed idea of the sexual charge motivating the narrator's real or supposed change: "...I suggest it might be terribly Freudian [as well as ecological]." How or why is left unanswered, which underscores the openness of the book to the simplest of readings (a "psychological" thriller), as well as more involved ones.
    6. See Anonymous (January 6, 1989) for a typically calm response to the potentially violent and jarring metamorphosis of the narrator. Such readings depend upon foregrounding the "surrealistic" elements of the novel; this reviewer is right to put her/his finger on the crux of the plot, which is "a metaphor for the fragility of holding on to one's identity." Disappointingly, this is not explored any further.
    7. The Kerry Babies case as described by Rosemary Mahoney: "Joanne Hayes, distraught and unmarried, choked her own baby after giving birth to it in her mother's home. The Hayes family alleged that the police had conducted unethical and abusive investigation and had invented 'evidence' to be used against Joanne" (Mahoney 1993, 177-178). Joanne Hayes was convicted of murder.
    8. McGahern does not say which Tolstoy play he originally adapted. I rely on what McGahern may or may not have been thinking in this section more than I have in previous chapters, for two reasons: first, the lack of critical commentary on the play; second, the great private importance McGahern himself places on the message within the play. If the "grand old

man" of rural Ireland, himself the owner of a farm, is turning from complex analyses of his society to a blanket condemnation, it will surely have great affect on his future works. It is far from certain whether this blanket condemnation is coming from McGahern; but the possibility is intriguing.

CONCLUSION

> ...give me a thumbnail sketch,
> give me a hint of a subject even
> and I can work wonders with it.
> --*The Dream of A Beast*

> Irish women...seem to see what needs
> to be done to work the system and at the
> same time subvert it as much
> and as well as they can (Mulvey 1992, 515).

At the end of this study, I would like to focus on two related aspects of the literary representations present in McGahern's and Jordan's fiction: the congruence of the two authors' ultimate messages, and the influence of this literature on the socio-political audience it reaches. The former reiterates the links between the two authors, their sense of the importance of female performance and their place in a canon of literature about performative resistance. The latter helps one to understand the import of this literature by situating it within its social context, and answers the questions about real women that are begged by a discussion of female characters.

I. Literary Links

Both Jordan and McGahern make overt calls for salvation in their more recent works, Jordan in *The Crying Game* and McGahern in *The Power of Darkness*. McGahern's latest title in particular, an ironic echo of his first novel, *The Dark*, gives one a sense that that rural darkness he had hoped would be lifted over the thirty years since that first publication has in fact triumphed over its opposition. Both authors seem to have come to place their faith in the efforts of those who suffer most from oppression, those most in need of salvation-- killers, wives, small farmers, and other struggling populations--to change the society which produces them. From invoking more mystical encounters as catalysts for change, from the internal journey of the imagination of *The Past*, and the all-out nebulousness of reality in *The Dream of A Beast*, to the all-too-human yet ultimately rewarding love relationships of *The Miracle* and *The Crying Game*; to the spiritual awakening of Moran at the end of *Amongst Women* and the brush with the origins of life found only through embracing death in *The Pornographer*, both authors have come to represent their average people turning to each other rather than to a source outside humanity in their later works. And the results of turning to each other for help are mixed.

The politics of the social milieu are much more pronounced in these later works; we see Jordan and McGahern representing social strife in much less metaphoric terms. On McGahern's farms, the growing economic development of the nation is no longer represented by the reluctant exodus of the children to the city, but by the commercialization of the farm itself. The farmer is become at last a businessman. Jordan's women move from mystically-empowered mothers to more flesh-and-blood, overtly constructed social beings negotiating their circumscribed role in a hostile society and valuing men as sympathetic companions rather than relying upon them as sons or husbands. And in this political world, the day-to-day grind of coping and resisting is unleavened by visions, spiritual visitations or transcendence of the body and its laws. The body's relation to politics is much more foregrounded, through abortion, gender construction, hostage-taking, prostitution, and forced marriage. No one rises above this sort of politicization as Rene O'Shaughnessy once did. These later characters must confront their society in more political ways.

This is not to say, however, that the earlier sort of resistance is invalidated by the latter kind. It is rather its natural extension, or development. The later works' more traditional political engagement is founded on the earlier works' re-statement of the political problem. In other words, because the earlier fiction brought to light the critical importance of feminine resistance and performance, the later fiction can take this performative resistance as a given in the more concrete political struggle for social change. So the earlier works define performance and the later works implement it. *Amongst Women* is an especially interesting work because it is on the borderline between the two sets; in Rose and Michael Moran's story we see the beginning of the modernization the farm and of its inhabitants, yet the Morans still respect, at least outwardly, the traditional politics--gender and social--

which marginalize feminine performance. The grey area of whether it is true reverence or merely lip-service which keeps Rose Moran and the other Moran women within the worship of the patriarch is the hallmark of the transitional nature of the story.

Of course, all the novels studied here are transitional to differing degrees. In this they are representative of the place and the era in which they were written, the Republic of Ireland from the 1950s to the 1980s, a period of extreme economic change (as I have documented above) which enabled social change even as it produced a traditional backlash against all kinds of change, but especially against social change as it pertained to modifying gender roles. But it is exactly in reaction to this backlash that the later works approach gender conflict with a much more materialist agenda. What Jimmy gets from his mother Renée during her brief return to his life is very different from what Fergus gains from his relationship with Dil. Both men set out desiring a woman to give them a sense of different possibilities for their programmatic lives; but where Jimmy gets what he needs from Renée and passes back out of her life, Fergus must give of himself, become entangled in Dil's political situation, in order to gain anything for himself. Of course, this is partially because Jimmy is a much younger man than Fergus, but then again, situating Jimmy as a youth is no accident in the text. The focus has shifted from male *bildungsroman* with woman as removed muse to a more engaged, interdependent relationship between men and women which is all about hard political choices. This is the performative aspect, again, of the writing. The removed, spiritual woman's counterpart was the essential man--in this way, Feminine helped inspire Masculine. This is rejected in favor of women whose performance of gender relations forces men to reconsider their one-sided, essentialist uses for women in their lives. The comparison is very similar when one looks at the difference between the pornographer's experience with his aunt (and, to a certain extent, the woman he gets pregnant) and Paul's relationship with Eileen in *The Power of Darkness*. Even within *The Pornographer*, however, the narrator has the beginnings of a more politically-engaged relationship with the nurse, one which demands that he re-evaluate his own politics as he encounters hers--from the negotiations over birth control to her insistence upon the equality of partners within marriage. Thus the frustrated desires of Una O'Shaughnessy are relieved to a certain extent by the next generation.

But only to a certain extent. There is no general sense of celebration in the progression of these works, most obviously because the long battle with the traditional state has just been engaged. But the work of the past has affected the audience for more engaged works--and in many ways it has had a substantial role in creating that audience, as we shall see below.

II. Literary Applications

The literary engagement with quotidian people and resistance is at once reflective of its readers and at work to create those readers. In Ireland, there is a close relation between literary women's resistance to the state which others them and actual political organization by women against that state. It is a small nation, where writers are often in close contact with "average people," and many political figures are avowed "average people" whose original neighborhood influence spread quickly to national levels after gaining press coverage in one of the few national daily papers, radio or television news programs. "Average" women can easily make headlines, as what are traditionally devalued as "women's issues" (save abortion rights) in other nations-- birth control, divorce law, equal pay--are mainstream concerns in Ireland. Many national leaders fighting repressive laws concerning women were not long before their political careers housewives who dared to speak out. It is their status as good wives and mothers which protects those women who organize against traditional laws, and it is that domestic identity which encourages other women to get involved.

This valuing of the domestic woman's role in society, apparently at odds with political change, is actually a continuation of Irish women's utilization of informal networks and organizations rather than charismatic, individual action to create change. Anne Mulvey points out that Irish women

> seem to have the ability to see and understand the power of authority and what's needed to placate it while simultaneously being pragmatic, anarchic, and radical in furthering their own goals. This may reflect the long tradition of colonization under British rule. It seems a natural response and effective survival strategy given the repressive forces [working in Irish society]...the University College Dublin Women's Studies Forum...followed the rules of propriety and decorum of this staid, conservative university setting apparently comfortably, while at the same time actively including and welcoming poor women ordinarily not even invited into many less

hierarchical settings...Being a feminist living under patriarchal institutions is a contradiction anywhere [but] in Ireland, given its tradition of living contradictions, there may be a greater ability to pay lipservice to authority while effecting real change. (Mulvey 1992, 515)

This tactic of conforming to one's social position while working to change it, so reminiscent of Rose Moran, is not simply one of deceit. The key to understanding this form of resistance is knowing that the women involved do not denigrate their domestic, traditional roles. They do not, for example, as a tenet of their resistance, pretend to accept motherhood while privately hating it. Rather, they emphasize how the positive value of motherhood is damaged by laws that take choice away from potential mothers and punish those who either choose not to have children or choose to have children outside the traditional nuclear-family setting. In this way Irish women stand protected by their societal position and by each other while re-writing the rules associated to the roles.

  This sort of community action is unique to Ireland as a western nation. Mulvey notes the differences between Irish and US and British women's studies organizations, illustrating how Irish women's groups are consistently more open to uneducated, domestic and older women than their western counterparts. Women come together in reading groups or even craft groups which evolve almost naturally into political action: the Coolock Adult Learning Group, for example, began as a literature appreciation group and "had gone from talking about their personal lives and experiences to participating in civil and reproductive rights campaigns. Some also joined a coalition of women's groups that organized a national conference on women and poverty" (511). What makes Irish women's political organization different from other western nations' groups is the sense that it is exactly traditional women themselves who, rather than representing the enemy, are most qualified to lead resistance against the mainstream, as they have supported it and suffered under it for decades. Their life experience is the social validation of their movements. President Mary Robinson was compelled to support her liberal stance on many issues by "emphasizing the importance of her role as Catholic mother and wife" (283). In 1983 Dublin housewife Ruth Riddick began giving out contraception information from her home and quickly became a household (albeit often dirty) word in Ireland. She is now a leading political activist working out of her

Dublin home (Mahoney 1993, 47). How her fame spread is archetypical of the almost underground, definitely common-ground structure of women's resistance in Ireland--her number was written on the doors and walls of hundreds of women's public bathrooms:

> I told Ruth about having found her phone number on a bathroom door. I told her how I had seen posters pasted up all over Dublin...with the number for abortion information written on them, and how the very next day, without fail, the posters would be ripped down or covered over with black paint.
> [Ruth responded] 'The bathroom walls...that's a wholly appropriate response of the women's movement, I think. But equally it horrifies me...I do not think it's appropriate that the most important decisions about women's lives should be conducted in toilets. Of course, it's quite right that the women's movement responds that way. You're left in a situation where you're dealing in informal networks, where you're dealing with people ringing you up who may have got your phone number from a *toilet..*' (her italics--65-66).

In other western nations, a women's movement forced to restrict (almost devote) itself to disseminating information with marking pens in bathrooms would hardly be considered a proper women's movement at all. In Ireland, it is recognized that no method of disseminating information can be disdained as worthless when the information is so precious, and so heavily policed.

This domestic power is not unnoticed by the government, of course. Housewife power is fully acknowledged, feared, and prosecuted. Young women who attend small political marches can expect to receive visits from the Special Branch of the police (equivalent to the FBI in the US), and their employers, once informed by the police of their female employees' activism, can terminate their employment (172-174). The domestic woman must be spiritually empowered only; her power in the home is not to be translated into self-determination. But what enables Irish women to lobby for change while valuing their domesticity is their understanding that their power comes from the home--figuratively, as the Wife and Mother is honored in traditional rhetoric, and literally, in the case of ownership. It is ironic that as Irish women transform the household from prison to asset by insisting upon their economic and political rights within it, repressive forces seek to keep them still by threatening their new-found sense of ownership, an issue which lurks behind other, seemingly unrelated issues such as divorce:

> Inheritance is what the whole divorce referendum was about. [The government] told the women of Ireland that their farms would be sold from under them if divorce became legal in Ireland. This debate went on for days on the radio. Older women would call up and say, 'Sure, 'twould be the death to us if we had divorce. Anytime he went down to the pub and saw a young one sitting there that he liked, that'd be the end of *us*'...[they] scared the women of Ireland by telling them that the farms would be sold out from under them (her italics - 187).

Like Rose Moran, Irish women are at once intimidated into obedience by and willing to fight to keep their homes. As Honor Fagan puts it, "To these women family life is central, because they believe their only status is located within it...In general the women speak of a tiredness, not a rebelliousness, with the servicing of their families. They all believe that their childrearing work is a good thing...but they are confused by the low status they experience" (Fagan 1991, 67). But if they are conditioned to accept "that a woman's life pattern must be predominantly home-centred" they are more and more able to use their conformity to this norm as political leverage (Robinson 1979, 58). As blamelessly feminine components of the state, they cannot be accused of anarchic intentions when they lobby for change, just as Una O'Shaughnessy's patriotic theater tableaux not only pave the way for her husband's status as a national hero but provide her with a safety net when she explores more scandalous avenues of society.

While women in literature do not blend in seamlessly with real women, literature in Ireland as in most nations provides an ideological context for legislation and preservation of social mores. When Eunice McCarthy points out when speaking of the Employment Equality Act of 1977, that "the vocational guidance counselor must come face to face with the fact that up to the present our sex role ideology has severely limited the number of alternatives that the female adolescent [is] *psychologically prepared to consider*," one cannot deny that literature and literary images play a large role in developing the sex role ideology and preparing the individual psychology involved in accepting that ideology (my italics--McCarthy 1979, 112). In a nation like the Republic of Ireland, where the national literature is a highly visible component of national self-image and the populace is small, literary consciousness-shaping is even more pronounced. A best-seller bought by a million people has reached over one-quarter of the total population. When Betty Purcell wonders at the end of her article describing how changes of men's and women's *attitudes* about women's rights have done little to affect the *reality* of discrimination against women—"how much apart from our consciousness of the problem has really changed?"--one can counter some of her pessimism by noting that changes in attitudes pave the way for how much actual change young people are "psychologically prepared to consider," and one must also acknowledge how much literature has had to do with those changes in attitude (Purcell 1980, 559). "Certainly literature has helped to erode the compact majorities that came to power in Ireland after 1921 and the censorships they brought with them," states Edna Longley (Longley 1994, 9).

No lengthy study has been made of the extent of the literary contribution to political and social change in Ireland. But it cannot be assumed that literature merely reflects what is already present in society. If this were so, McGahern's strong women of the 1950s and 1960s would not have had to have been so carefully embedded within a patriarchal narrative. And Jordan's experimental texts dealing with blurred gender lines and magical mothers would not have been deemed more English than Irish by Irish critics. The women in McGahern's and Jordan's texts are, as Irish women, at once ahead of their time and monitors of actual change. As real women make small gains in political power, McGahern and Jordan create new women, just a little ahead of their readers, working out the ethical and moral consequences of the changes they are both anticipating and, to a lesser yet important extent, representing.

Their work has also opened the door to new novels which confront gender issues on a much more confident and obvious level, such as Nina FitzPatrick's *Fables of the Irish Intelligentsia* and Timothy O'Grady's *Motherland*. Contemporary Anglo-Irish literature has begun to abandon its conservative, national role and is now providing public opinion with images of gender relations which are leaps ahead of the immediate reality--or, in many cases, the desires--of its audience. Neil Jordan's groundbreaking work in this respect is crucial to any understanding of the changes taking place in Anglo-Irish fiction, and Jordan's work is, as I hope to have shown, intimately linked to John McGahern's painstaking opening up of the traditional novel to "women's issues." Ireland still lags behind in making good on its original promises to women, but its literature is finally catching up by realizing its revolutionary potential.

Bibliography

Allen, Michael and Angela Wilcox, eds. 1989. *Critical Approaches to Anglo-Irish Literature*. Totowa: Barnes and Noble Books.

Anonymous. 1966. Hit Him Again, He's Irish. Review of *The Dark*, by John McGahern. *Time*, 87 (February 18): 103.

---. 1982. Review of *The Past*, by Neil Jordan. *The Observer* (June 20): 31.

---. 1979. Review of *The Pornographer*, by John McGahern. *The Observer* (October 14): 39.

---. 1980. Review of *The Pornographer*, by John McGahern. *The Observer* (October 5): 128.

---. 1965. Swotting out of the Farm. Review of *The Dark*, by John McGahern. *Times Literary Supplement*, 3298 (May 13): 365.

Ayearst, Morley. 1970. *The Republic of Ireland: Its Government and Politics*. New York: NYU Press.

Barra, Allen. 1990. Here Comes Mr. Jordan. *American Film* 15:4 (January): 36-41.

---. 1991. Jordan Airs. *The Village Voice* 36:32 (6 August): 63.

Battersby, Eileen. 1992. Tragic, Tormented World. *Fortnight* 312 (December): 44-45.

Beale, Jenny. 1987. *Women in Ireland: Voices of Change.* Bloomington: Indiana UP.

Berlind, Bruce. 1981. Review of *The Pornographer*, by John McGahern. *New Letters: A Magazine of Fine Writing* 47:4 (Summer): 140-141.

Bland, Elizabeth L. 1993. Queuing for *The Crying Game. Time* 141:4 (January): 63.

Boyce, D. George. 1982. *Nationalism in Ireland.* Baltimore: Johns Hopkins UP.

Boyd, Ernest. 1992. *Ireland's Literary Renaissance.* New York: A. A. Knopf.

Breen, Richard, et al. 1990. *Understanding Contemporary Ireland: State, Class and Development in the Republic of Ireland.* Basingstoke: Macmillan.

Brown, Georgia. 1992. Unforgettable. Review of *The Crying Game*, by Neil Jordan. *The Village Voice* 37:48 (December): 24.

Brown, Terence. 1988. *Ireland's Literature.* Totowa: Barnes and Noble Books.

---. 1922. *Ireland: A Social and Cultural History, 1922 to the Present.* Ithaca: Cornell UP.

Burton, Joan, et al. 1994. Divorce and Reality. *Fortnight* 329 (June): 14-19.

Butler, Judith. 1993. *Bodies that Matter: On the Discursive Limits of "Sex."* New York: Routledge.

Cahalan, James. 1983. *Great Hatred, Little Room: The Irish Historical Novel.* Syracuse: Syracuse UP

---. 1989. *The Irish Novel: A Critical History*. Boston: Iona College Press.

Cahill, Thomas. 1995. *How the Irish Saved Civilization: The Untold Story of Ireland's Heroic Role from the Fall of Rome to the Rise of Medieval Europe*. New York: Anchor Doubleday.

Cairnes, David and Shaun Richards. 1988. *Writing Ireland: Colonialism, Nationalism and Culture*. Manchester: Manchester UP.

Carpenter, Andrew, ed. 1977. Introduction. *Place, Personality and the Irish Writer*. Irish Literary Studies 1 Bucks: Colin Smythe.

Chow, Rey. 1991. *Woman and Chinese Modernity: The Politics of Reading Between West and East*. Minneapolis: University of Minnesota Press.

Clancy, Mary. 1990. Aspects of Women's Contribution to the Oireachtas Debate in the Irish Free State, 1922-1937. *Women Surviving: Studies in Irish Women's History in the 19th and 20th Centuries*. Dublin: Poolbeg Press, Ltd.

Clancy, Patrick, et al. 1986. *Ireland: A Sociological Profile*. Dublin: Institute of Public Administration.

Clapp, Susannah. 1979. Catching Up: Fiction. Review of *Night in Tunisia and Other Stories*, by Neil Jordan. *Times Literary Supplement* 4001 (November 23): 42.

Clark, J. P. 1992. The First Doing: A Nigerian Encounter with Irish Literature. Edited Joseph McMinn. *The Internationalism of Irish Literature and Drama*. Irish Literary Studies 41. Bucks: Colin Smythe.

Connolly, Peter, ed. 1982. Introduction. *Literature and the Changing Ireland*. Irish Literary Studies 9 Bucks: Colin Smythe.

Cook, Bruce. 1975. The Irish: Pugnacious, powerless and bored. Review of *The Leavetaking* by John McGahern. *National Observer* 14 (March 1): 21.

Cox, Shelley. 1980. Review of *The Past*, by Neil Jordan. *Library Journal* 105:19 (November 1): 2345.

Craig, Patricia. 1982. Paperback Fiction in Brief. Review of *The Past*, by Neil Jordan. *Times Literary Supplement* (August 13): 888.

Cronin, John. 1992. John McGahern's *Amongst Women*: Retrenchment and Renewal. *Irish University Review* 22:1 (Spring): 168-176.

Davies, Miranda, ed. 1983. *Third World--Second Sex: Women's Struggles and National Liberation--Third World Women Speak Out.* London: Zed Press.

Deane, Seamus. 1986. *A Short History of Irish Literature.* Notre Dame: University of Notre Dame Press.

Deane, Seamus. 1990. Introduction *to Nationalism, Colonialism, and Literature*, by Edward Said. Minneapolis: University of Minnesota Press.

Edwards, Page. 1980. Review of *Night in Tunisia and Other Stories* by Neil Jordan. *Library Journal* 105:5 (March 1): 637.

Fagan, G. Honor. 1991. Local Struggles: Women in the Home and Critical Feminist Pedagogy in Ireland. *Journal of Education* 173:1: 65-75.

Fallis, Richard. 1977. *The Irish Renaissance.* Syracuse: Syracuse UP.

Fisher, Emma. 1979. Review of *Night in Tunisia and Other Stories*, by Neil Jordan. *Spectator* 242:724 (April 21): 28.

FitzPatrick, Nina. 1991. *Fables of the Irish Intelligentsia*. London: Penguin.

Flanagan, Thomas. 1959. *The Irish Novelists, 1800-1850*. New York: Columbia University Press.

Fleischmann, Ruth. 1992. The Insularity of Irish Literature: Cultural Subjugation and the Difficulties of Reconstruction. Edited Joseph McMinn. *The Internationalism of Irish Literature and Drama*. Irish Literary Studies 41. Bucks: Colin Smythe.

Foster, John Wilson. 1987. *Fictions of the Irish Literary Revival: A Changeling Art*. Syracuse: Syracuse UP.

Frever, Grattan. 1983. Change Naturally: The Fiction of O'Flaherty, O'Faolain, McGahern. *Eire-Ireland* 18:1 (Spring): 138-144.

Gaitskell, Deborah and Elaine Unterhalter. 1989. Mothers of the Nation: A Comparative Analysis of Nation, Race and Motherhood in Afrikaner Nationalism and the African National Congress. Edited Nira Yval-Davies, et al. *Woman Nation-State*. New York: St. Martin's Press, 1989.

Giles, Jeff. 1993. *The Crying Game* Star Jaye Davidson Breaks the Silence. *Rolling Stone* 653 (April 1): 36-39,59,65.

Gitzen, Julian. 1991. Wheels Along the Shannon: The Fiction of John McGahern. *Journal of Irish Literature* 20:3 (September): 36-49.

Glicksman, Marlaine. 1990. Neil Jordan's Angel Heart: Irish Eyes. *Film Comment* 26:1 (January): 9-11, 68.

Hadfield, Andrew. 1992. Anglo-Irish Literature: Definitions and (False) Origins. Edited Joseph McMinn. *The Internationalism of Irish Literature and Drama*. Irish Literary Studies 41 Bucks: Colin Smythe.

Harmon, Maurice. 1985. The Era of Inhibitions: Irish Literature 1920-1960. Edited Sekine Masaru. *Irish Writers and Society at Large*. Irish Literary Studies 22 Totowa: Barnes and Noble Books.

Harris, Mark. 1993. The Crying Game: The Little Movie that Could. *Entertainment Weekly* 157 (February 12): 17-21.

Hawkins, Maureen S. G. 1992. *An Giall, The Hostage*, and *Kongi's Harvest*: Post-Colonial Irish, Anglo-Irish and Nigerian variations on a Post-modern Theme. Edited Joseph McMinn. *The Internationalism of Irish Literature and Drama*. Irish Literary Studies 41. Bucks: Colin Smythe.

Hearty, K. B. 1992. Review of *The Crying Game*, by Neil Jordan. *Premiere* 6:4 (December): 36.

Hogan, Robert. 1984. Old Boys, Young Bucks and New Women: The Contemporary Irish Short Story. Edited James F. Kilroy. *The Irish Short Story: A Critical History*. New York: G. K. Hall and Co.

Hoppen, K. Theodore. 1988. *Ireland Since 1800: Conflict and Conformity*. London: Longman Press.

Howe, Parkman. 1975. Oddly enough, it was a good year for Irish writers. Review of *The Leavetaking*, by John McGahern. *Christian Science Monitor* 67:230 (October 22): 18.

Innes, Catherine. 1990. *The Devil's Own Mirror: The Irishman and the African in Modern Literature*. Washington, DC: Three Continents Press.

---. 1993. *Woman and Nation in Irish Literature and Society, 1880-1935*. Athens: University of Georgia Press.

Irwin, Michael. 1978. Sorrowful Pipings. Review of *Getting Through*, by John McGahern. *Times Literary Supplement* 3967 (June 16): 663.

Jayawardena, Kumari. 1986. *Feminism and Nationalism in the Third World*. London: Zed Books, Ltd..

Jeffares, A. Norman. 1982. *Anglo-Irish Literature*. New York: Schocken Books.

Jones, D.A.N. 1983. Review of *The Dream of A Beast*, by Neil Jordan. *London Review of Books* 5:19 (October 20): 17-18.

Jones, Lewis. 1984. Pyromania. Review of *The Dream of A Beast*, by Neil Jordan. *Spectator* 252:8113 (January 7): 20-21.

Jordan, Neil. 1980. *The Past*. New York: George Braziller.

---. 1980. *Night in Tunisia*. New York: George Braziller.

---. 1990. *The Miracle*. London: Palace Productions.

---. 1991. Interview by Liane Hansen. All Things Considered. NPR, July 21.

---. 1993. *The Crying Game*. In *A Neil Jordan Reader*. New York: Vintage International.

---. 1993. *The Dream of A Beast*. In *A Neil Jordan Reader*. New York, Vintage International.

Keane, Patrick J. 1988. *Yeats, Joyce, Ireland and the Myth of the Devouring Female*. Columbia: University of Missouri Press.

Kenneally, Michael, ed. 1988. *Cultural Contexts and Literary Idioms in Contemporary Irish Literature*. Bucks: Colin Smythe.

Kennedy, Eileen. 1983. The Novels of John McGahern: The Road Away Becomes the Road Back. Edited James D. Brophy and Raymond Porter. *Contemporary Irish Writing*. Boston: Iona College Press, 1983.

Kennedy, Liam. 1992/1993. Modern Ireland: Post-Colonial Society or Post-Colonial Pretensions? *The Irish Review* 13 (Winter): 107-121.

Kilroy, James F., ed. 1984. Introduction. *The Irish Short Story: A Critical History*. Boston: G.K. Hall and Company.

---. 1984. Setting the Standards: Writers of the 20s and 30s. *The Irish Short Story: A Critical History*. Boston: G.K. Hall and Company.

Kirby, Peadar. 1988. *Has Ireland a Future?* Dublin and Cork: The Mercier Press.

Kythreotis, Anna. 1986. When Fame is a Necessary Evil. Review of *The Past*, by Neil Jordan. *The New York Times* 141:12 (September 6): 16.

Lee, Hermione. 1990. A domestic history of Ireland. Review of *Amongst Women*, by John McGahern. *The Independent on Sunday* (May 6,): 17.

Lee, Joseph. 1991. The Irish Constitution of 1937. *Ireland's Histories: Aspects of State, Society and Ideology*. Ed. Seán Hutton and Paul Stewart. London: Routledge.

Lloyd, David. 1993. *Anomalous States: Irish Writing and the Post-Colonial Moment*. Durham: Duke UP.

---. 1992. Violence and the Constitution of the Novel. *Meanjin* 51:4 (Summer): 751-765.

Lloyd, Richard. 1987. The Symbolic Mass: Thematic Resolution in the Irish Novels of John McGahern. *Emporia State Research Studies* 36:2 (Fall): 5-23.

Longley, Edna. 1994. *The Living Stream: Literature and Revisionism in Ireland*. Newcastle upon Tyne: Bloodaxe Books.

Luddy, Maria and Cliona Murphy. 1990. 'Cherchez la Femme:' The Elusive Woman in Irish History. Edited Maria Luddy and Cliona Murphy. *Women Surviving: Studies in Irish Women's History in the 19th and 20th Centuries*. Dublin: Poolbeg Press, Ltd.

Mahoney, Rosemary. 1993. *Whoredom in Kimmage: Irish Women Coming of Age*. Boston: Houghton Mifflin Company.

Mano, D. Keith. 1980. Private Parts. Review of *The Pornographer*, by John McGahern. *National Review* 32:3 (February 8): 167-168.

Manning, Maurice. 1979. Women in Irish National and Local Politics 1922-77. Edited Margaret MacCurtain and Donncha Ó Corrain. *Women in Irish Society: The Historic Dimension*. Dublin: Arlen House.

Mantel, Hilary. 1988. Review of *High Spirits*, by Neil Jordan. *Spectator* 261:8372 (December 24): 89.

Martin, Augustine. 1970. Literature and Society, 1938-1951. Ed. Kevin B. Nowlan and T. Desmond Williams. *Ireland in the War Years and After*. Notre Dame: University of Notre Dame Press.

McCarthy, Eunice. 1979. Women and Work in Ireland: The Present, and preparing for the Future. Edited Margaret MacCurtain and Donncha Ó Corrain. *Women in Irish Society: The Historic Dimension*. Dublin: Arlen House.

McGahern, John. 1966. *The Dark*. New York: A. A. Knopf.

---. 1979. *The Pornographer*. New York: Harper.

---. 1990. *Amongst Women*. London: Faber and Faber.

---. 1991.*The Power of Darkness*. London: Faber and Faber.

---. 1993. Toward a Community of Cultures: "Minority Culture." *World Press Review* 40:1 (January): 24.

McHugh, Roger and Maurice Harmon. 1982. *Short History of Anglo-Irish Literature, from its Origins to the Present Day*. Totowa: Barnes and Noble Books.

McIlroy, Brian. 1988. *World Cinema 4: Ireland*. Trowbridge: Flicks Books.

McMinn, Joe. 1989. Review of *The Irish Novel* by James Cahalan. *Fortnight* 273:23 : 40.

Mellors, John. 1980. Harsh Winds. Review of *The Past*, by Neil Jordan. *The Listener* 104:2690 (November 6): 623.

---. 1983. Sun-stunned Vacuum. Review of *The Dream of A Beast*, by Neil Jordan. *The Listener* 110:2986 (October 13): 31.

---. 1978. Leg Irons. Review of *Getting Through*, by John McGahern. *The Listener* 99:2565 (June): 818-819.

Mudrick, Marvin. 1966. Evelyn, Get the Horseradish. Review of *The Dark*, by John McGahern. *Hudson Review* 19:2 (Summer): 305, 311-314.

Mullin, Molly. 1991. Representations of History, Irish Feminism, and the Politics of Difference. *Feminist Studies* 17:1 (Spring): 29-50.

Mulvey, Anne. 1992. Irish Women's Studies and Community Activism: Reflections and Exemplars. *Women's Studies International Forum* 15:4 (July): 507-516.

Murphy, Cliona. 1989. *The Women's Suffrage Movement and Irish Society in the Early Twentieth Century.* Philadelphia: Temple UP.

Nairn, Tom. 1988. *The Enchanted Glass: Britain and its Monarchy.* London: Hutchinson Radius.

Naughton, John. 1979. Dirty Dublin. Review of *The Pornographer*, by John McGahern. *The Listener* 107:2731 (October 18): 534-535.

O'Connell, Shaun. 1984. Door into the Light: John McGahern's Ireland. *The Massachusetts Review* 25:2 (Summer): 255-268.

O'Grady, Timothy. 1991. *Motherland.* New York: Anchor Doubleday.

O'Neill, Catherine. 1979. Review of *The Pornographer*, by John McGahern. *The New Republic* 181:24 (December 15): 39-40.

O'Neill, Daniel J. 1987. Enclave Nation-Building: The Irish Experience. *Journal of Ethnic Studies* 15:3 (Fall): 1-25.

O'Toole, Fintan. 1988. Island of Saints and Silicon: Literature and Social Change in Contemporary Ireland. Edited Richard Kenneally. *Cultural Contexts and Literary Idioms in Contemporary Ireland.* Bucks: Colin Smythe.

---. 1990. Both completely Irish and universal. *The Irish Times* (September 15): 5.

---. 1990. The family as independent republic. *The Irish Times* (October 13): 2.

Owens, Rosemary Cullen. 1984. *Smashing Times: A History of the Irish Women's Suffrage Movement.* Dublin: Attic Press.

Paulin, Tom. 1980. The Fire-Monster. Review of *The Pornographer*, by John McGahern. *Encounter* 54:1 (January): 60-62.

Powers, John. 1986. I got my job through Channel 4. *American Film* 10 (July-August): 48-49.

Prescott, Peter S. 1979. Adventures in the Skin Trade. Review of *The Pornographer*, by John McGahern. *Newsweek* 94 (November 5): 107-108.

---. 1971. Desperate Men. Review of *Nightlines*, by John McGahern. *Newsweek* 77 (February 8): 91-92.

---. 1975. Super Soap. Review of *The Leavetaking*, by John McGahern. *Newsweek* 85 (February 17): 90-92.

Purcell, Betty. 1980. 10 Years of Progress? Some Statistics. *Crane Bag Book of Irish Studies* 4:1: 556-559.

Quinn, Antoinette. 1991. A Prayer for my Daughters: Patriarchy in *Amongst Women*. *Canadian Journal of Irish Studies* 17:1: 79 90.

Quinn, Gerard. 1970. The Changing Pattern of Irish Society, 1938-1951. Edited Kevin B. Nowlan and T. Desmond Williams. *Ireland in the War Years and After*. Notre Dame: University of Notre Dame Press.

Rafroidi, Patrick. 1982. Change and the Irish Imagination. Edited Peter Connolly. *Literature and the Changing Ireland*. Irish Literary Studies 9 Totowa: Barnes and Noble Books.

Robinson, Mary. 1979. Women and the New Irish State. Edited Margaret MacCurtain and Donncha Ó Corrain. *Women in Irish Society: The Historical Dimension*. Dublin: Arlen House.

Rockett, Kevin, et al, eds. 1987. *Cinema and Ireland*. Syracuse: Syracuse UP.

Sawyer, Roger. 1993. *We are but Women: Women in Ireland's History.* London: Routledge.

Schwartz, Kalheinz. 1984. John McGahern's Point of View. *Eire-Ireland* 19:3 (Fall): 92-110.

Shackelton, Robert and Ray Sawhill. 1989. Here Comes Mr. Jordan. *Interview* 19:12 (December): 74-76.

Simmons, James. 1974. *Ten Irish Poets: An Anthology of Poems by George Buchanan, et al.* Cheadle Hulme: Carcanet Press.

Stein, Benjamin. 1993. The Crying Game. *American Spectator* 26:3 (March): 44-47.

Steinberg, Sybil. 1989. Review of *The Dream of A Beast*, by Neil Jordan. *Publisher's Weekly* 235:1 (January 6): 89.

Story, R. O. 1986. The Cult of *The Crying Game*. *New York Magazine* 26:4 (January 25): 36-39.

Suleri, Sara. 1992. *The Rhetoric of English India.* Chicago: The University of Chicago Press.

Sweetman, Rosita. 1979. *On Our Backs: Sexual Attitudes in a Changing Ireland.* London: Pan Books, Ltd..

Taheri, Amir. 1988. *The Cauldron: The Middle East Behind the Headlines.* London: Hutchinson Ltd.

Taylor, Estella Ruth. 1969. *The Modern Irish Writers: Crosscurrents of Criticism.* New York: Greenwood Press.

Taylor, Paul. 1980. The Light of the World. Review of *The Past*, by Neil Jordan. *Times Literary Supplement* 4050 (November 14): 1280.

Thompson, William. 1967. *The Imagination of an Insurrection: Dublin, Easter 1916, A Study of an Ideological Movement.* New York: Oxford University Press.

Toolan, Michael J. 1981. John McGahern: The Historian and the Pornographer. *The Canadian Journal of Irish Studies* 7:2 (December): 39-55.

Vivante, Paolo. 1991. McGahern and the Homeric Moment. *Canadian Journal of Irish Studies* 17:1 (July): 53-56.

Wade, Rosalind. 1981. Review of *The Past*, by Neil Jordan. *Contemporary Review* 238:1381 (January): 45.

Walby, Sylvia. 1992. Women and Nation. Edited Anthony D. Smith. *Ethnicity and Nationalism.* London: E. J. Brill.

Ward, Margaret. 1983. *Unmanageable Revolutionaries: Women and Irish Nationalism.* London: Pluto Press, Ltd.

Warner, Alan. 1981. The Growth of Anglo-Irish Literature. *A Guide to Anglo-Irish Literature.* New York: St. Martin's Press.

Welch, Robert. 1985. Some Thoughts on Writing a Companion to Irish Literature. Edited Sekine Masaru. *Irish Writers and Society at Large.* Irish Literary Studies 22 Totowa: Barnes and Noble Books.

Wiehe, Janet. 1979. Review of *The Pornographer*, by John McGahern. *Library Journal* 104:19 (December 15): 2665.

Index

Agency, 11, 58

Amongst Women, 42-48, 57, 74-84

    criticism of, 49-53

    references to, 117, 120, 122

Anglo-Irish

    culture, 2, 3-9, 10, 11, 13, 15n2, 23, 27, 120-124

    female characters in literature, 26-28

    general literature, 1-7, 11, 13, 97n5, 120-124

    novel, 3-9, 11, 13-14, 15n5, 28, 132

Citizenship

    women and, 12, 14, 20, 22-28, 32n12

Colonialism, general 1-2, 19, 21, 25, 27, 29

    gender and, 27-29, 31n2,

Irish experience of, 2, 5-7, 9, 19, 21, 25

Irish novel and, 4-5

Crying Game, The, 84-96

    references to, 65, 107-108, 122n4, 125, 126

De-colonization, 10-12, 14, 19, 21, 56

de Valera, Eamon, 23, 31n6, 33n12, 44, 53

Dream of A Beast, The, 105-112, 122n3, 126

Essence,

    Amongst Women and, 51-53

    The Crying Game and, 96

    gender and, 28, 30, 33, 35, 44

    Irishness and, 19, 27, 31,

    The Miracle and, 57-58, 60-64

    nationalism, 7, 12-13

    The Past and, 38-42

Ethnicity, 2, 8-12, 38, 53, 56, 90-92

    gender in, 13, 26-27, 39-40, 44, 49-51

Family,

Amongst Women and, 45-51, 54-55, 80-88

Anglo-Irish novel and, 11, 14, 28, 33n16, 52, 54-55, 56, 102n2, 129

gender roles in, 29-30, 35, 131

Irish government policy toward, 24-27

The Miracle and, 59-67

The Past and, 40-44

The Pornographer and, 69-71

The Power of Darkness and, 113-122

Female:

The Crying Game and, 96-98

The Dream of A Beast and, 107-112

Irish government policy toward, 14, 26-28

Irish society and, 128-133

in literature, 14, 52, 56, 74

performance, 13-14, 30, 35, 44, 60, 66, 73, 86-88, 105

see also performance

The Power of Darkness and, 113-122

Feminine political identity, 13, 27, 50, 52, 54, 93, 108, 131

Feminization, 53-54, 95, 105, 108, 110-112

Free State, 7, 9, 19, 45, 46, 48-49

and women, 11, 23-27, 33n12

Gender,

in Anglo-Irish literature, 52, 56, 76, 88

in Irish society, 126-127, 132

Irish government and, 26-27

    in *The Crying Game*, 90-102

    in *The Dream of A Beast*, 108, 111-112

    in *The Power of Darkness*, 116-117, 118, 121

Grassroots action and literature, 128-133

History, Irish, 1-2, 6, 7, 9, 11, 15n1, 17n7, 21

    women's, 28, 32n8, 32n11, 33n14

Irishness, 1, 3-10, 12, 15, 19, 27

    The Past and, 40-41, 46, 56, 57n7

Identity, 1, 27, 38, 41, 56, 65, 72

    The Crying Game and, 89-102, 103n4

    gender and, 9-11, 39, 42-44, 73, 77, 108, 119, 122n6, 128

    Irish national, 1, 3, 9-11, 13-14, 49-51

    post-colonial, 6, 9, 35, 52

Joyce, James, 1, 3-4, 7

Jordan, Neil, 3, 10-11, 14-15, 19, 29-31, 125-126, 132

Marriage ban, 26

Masculine identity, 30, 54-55, 97, 103n6, 108, 116, 127

    masculinized, 14, 44, 97

McGahern, John, 3, 10-11, 14-15, 19, 29-31, 125-126, 132

Miracle, The, 59-67, 73, 76n1, 107

Nationalism, 20, 75

    Irish, 4-7, 14, 36

Nation-building, 2-3, 6, 10-13, 19-20, 29, 35, 37-38, 89

Nature, 2, 12, 25, 40, 52-56, 63, 66-67, 74, 91-92, 102-103, 107-108

Naturalization, 13, 35, 56

O'Faolain, Julia, 14, 33n15

Performance, 12-13, 26, 29, 49, 53

    Irish women and, 126-128

        in *Amongst Women*, 41-44, 47, 80, 85, 88

        in *The Crying Game*, 93, 94, 95-97

        in *The Dream of A Beast*, 105, 108, 117

        in *The Miracle*, 56, 57, 59, 60, 62-64

        in *The Past*, 27-28

        in *The Pornographer*, 70-72

        in *The Power of Darkness*, 118, 121, 123

Performative gender, 12, 14-15, 27-30, 35, 40, 47, 52, 67, 75, 102, 125-127

Pornographer, The, 67-73

    criticism of, 58n7, 74-75

    references to, 45, 55, 59, 76n5, 88, 116, 117, 120, 126, 127

Post-colonial, 2-3, 19-20

gender and, 12-15, 21, 25, 56

Irish experience of, 5-6, 9, 11, 19, 44

literature and, 10-11, 14, 86, 89

Power of Darkness, The, 105, 113-122, 125, 127

Purity, 12-13, 19, 27, 46, 52-53, 56, 69

Race, 5, 7-8, 21, 58, 103n5, 103n7

The Crying Game and, 89-91, 93, 96-99, 101

Republic of Ireland, 3, 5, 10-12, 14, 15n1, 19, 44, 56, 81

gender and, 22-24, 26, 33n13

Resistance, 5, 14, 31n6, 75, 99, 102n1

Irish women's, 12-13, 20, 44, 69-71, 97

domestic, 77, 81, 128-130

performative, 22, 30, 35, 75, 125-126, 128

Robinson, Mary, 6, 129-131

Sexuality, 13, 26, 54, 85, 95-96, 101

Third World, 5-6, 20

Tone, 5, 7-9, 15, 58n7

OHIO UNIVERSITY LIBRARY

Please return this book as soon as you have finished with it. In order to avoid a fine it must be returned by the latest date stamped below. All books are subject to recall after two weeks or immediately if needed for reserve.

OCT 23 2003
OCT 23 2003

CF